THOMAS JEI

Biograpl

Legacy of the Founaing Father

Gilbert N Harroald

TABLE OF CONTENTS

Introduction

Chapter 1: All Politics Is Local:Virginia to Philadelphia

Chapter 2: War and Revolution in Virginia

Chapter 3: Revolution in France

Chapter 4: Interregnum

Chapter 5: Secretary of State

Chapter 6: In Waiting

Chapter 7: Mr. President

Chapter 8: Disappointment: The Second Term

Chapter 9: Declining Years

INTRODUCTION

Thomas Jefferson died the day after the Fourth of July, from wasting diarrhea and a urinary tract infection. "Is it the Fourth?" he said at the end. On the same day, John Adams, his major opponent, died in Quincy, Massachusetts. His final words were, "Thomas Jefferson still lives," or, at the very least, "Thomas Jefferson..." Many stories of prominent men's dying words are apocryphal or pious fabrications, but these appear to be reasonably well substantiated. Jefferson addressed the major issues in his political life in the preceding letter. He didn't need to cite his personal authorship of the Declaration, the preamble to which had established the concept of human rights as the foundation for a republic for the first time in history. He vehemently reaffirmed his belief that the American Revolution was founded on international ideas and was thus unmistakably for export. He emphasized the importance of science and invention as the driving forces behind the Enlightenment, and mocked mere faith and credulous. His outspoken skepticism about religion is all the more startling considering that he had previously drafted his own will, planned his own tombstone, and told his doctors that he was well prepared to die.

When Lincoln later pondered whether the American ideal might last in his Gettysburg address, he directed his moral focus on Jefferson's Declaration of Independence ("four score and seven years" before 1863) rather than the federal Constitution. And this was quite kind of him. If one now looks approvingly at the sentences in Jefferson's closing message that denounce the idea of some humans being born with saddles and others with spurs, one also knows that Jefferson himself only needed to look out his own windows to see hereditary servitude in action. He purposefully delayed confronting this atrocity, and consciously deeded it as part of his legacy to future generations. One hundred and seventeen years after Jefferson's death, the dead and injured at Gettysburg (an fight on the eve of the Fourth of July) established a new record for atrocity in modern warfare.

Yet, without Jefferson's efforts, there would have been no grand Union to fight, even if it was "half-slave and half-free," for Lincoln and Douglas, and then Lincoln and Davis, and finally Grant and Lee. On July 4, 1803, the National Intelligencer of Washington published the news of the Louisiana Purchase, perhaps the greatest land deal in history, in which Napoleon Bonaparte agreed to sell to the United States everything between the Mississippi River and the Rocky Mountains—a tract of land then uncharted in terms of its full northern extent. This transaction, the result of skillful covert diplomacy and some deft short-circuiting of Congress and the Constitution, did not so much increase as it did reshape the United States, doubling its existing land area at a cost of four cents per acre. Later that day, Colonel Merriwether Lewis received his last letter of credit from President Jefferson and prepared to embark on the most audacious Enlightenment expedition ever envisioned, let alone attempted. The Fourth of July, 1803, deserves a higher place on the list of pivotal events or critical dates in human history. However, it was not a date on which anything actually occurred. Rather, it was a day when one meticulous plan was completed and another was inaugurated. Modern and postmodern historians like to use phrases like "inventing America" or "imagining America." It would be more accurate to say of Thomas Jefferson that he designed or authored America.

Given this, it would be either lazy or apparent to claim that he contained contradictions or paradoxes. This applies to everyone and everything. It would be far more remarkable to come across a historical figure, or even a country, that was not bound to this law. Jefferson was not a contradiction. Jefferson was a contradiction, and this can be observed at every stage of the story that is his life.

Chapter 1:
All Politics Is Local: Virginia to Philadelphia

Thomas Jefferson was born on April 13, 1743 (April 2 before the adoption of the Gregorian calendar in 1758), the son of stable planter stock in Virginia's native aristocracy. Peter Jefferson, his father, was a surveyor and cartographer whose parents were claimed to have immigrated from the Snowdonia district of northern Wales. Peter's marriage to Jane Randolph, whose family was one of the "names" of traditional Virginia society, could only benefit him. Perhaps it was his obvious contempt and dislike for his mother, to whom he almost never alluded, or his apparent indifference to aristocracy, but when he came to write his own very brief Autobiography in 1821, he spoke of bloodline and provenance and "pedigree," especially in his mother's case, with an affected indifference. "Let everyone ascribe the faith and merit he chooses to such trivial questions," he wrote. Since Jefferson always based American claims of right on the ancient Saxon autonomy allegedly established by the nearmythical English kings Hengist and Horsa, who had left Saxony and established a form of self-rule in southern England (he even wished to see their imagined likeness on the first Great Seal of the United States), we are confronted with his fondness for, if not necessity for, the negation of one of his positions by another.

When a young man appears to revere his father but is indifferent to his mother, we cannot hope to see very far beyond the opaque veil that is constantly present (and also not present). However, the nature of individual humans is not radically different, and it is not surprising that the adolescent Thomas considered himself inclined to go to seed and squander his time on loose company at one point. We also have an excruciating account of a "bad date" at the Raleigh Tavern's Apollo Room when, nerving himself to make approaches to the much sought-after Rebecca Burwell, he made a complete mess of the approach and made a more or less complete fool of himself. ("Good God!" he said the next morning to a buddy. Later, learning that Miss Burwell, a classmate's sister and the daughter of a family estate in York County, was engaged to another man, gave young Thomas the first of many migraine headaches that afflicted him periodically throughout his life.) This initial reversal was unquestionably painful. It is also undeniable that it was followed by another blunder, when he made a crude and futile attempt to seduce the wife of his friend John Walker. This is significant because it shows that Jefferson was fiery by nature when it came to girls, but was also made hesitant and cautious by experience. This is important to understand from the outset, and it would be unnecessary to do so if it weren't for the generations of historians who have written, up to the present day, as if he were not a male mammal at all.

Jefferson's time at William and Mary College in Williamsburg between 1760 and 1762 made the difference. He had the best luck a young man could have here, in that he was fortunate with his teachers. He became acquainted with Dr. William Small, a Scots-born instructor of the scientific method, and with the famous George Wythe, who taught law as an element of history, logic, and humanism and appears to have adopted the young man as a personal protégé. Once kindled, Jefferson's thirst for knowledge remained unquenchable for the rest of his life, as unappealing as his desire for the possession of books and the acquisition of their contents. Lord Bolingbroke, a pioneer critic of organized Christianity, was among the authors whose work he absorbed at the time. For anyone who was even remotely tuned in at the time, the air was thick with Enlightenment ideas, sweeping in from England, Scotland, and France. (Among other things, it was to transport Thomas Paine across the Atlantic with a letter of introduction from the learned Dr. Benjamin Franklin.) Jefferson never made a showy renunciation of religion, but his early alienation from its mystical or "revealed" parts would present itself throughout his mature life.

The demands of family and status demanded that this vulpine creature marry well, and he did so in 1772 with Martha Wayles Skelton, who was five years his junior. She became mistress of Monticello, sharing her husband's love of music (he had learnt the violin when he was nine years old). An worrisome hint appears here: a few months before his wedding, he wrote to one of his in-laws, Robert Skipwith, recommending Locke, Montesquieu, Hume, and other Enlightenment authors to him while also strongly endorsing Lawrence Sterne. This support is expressed even more emphatically in a 1787 letter to his cousin Peter Carr, in which Jefferson refers to Sterne's work as "the best course of morality that ever was written." We also know that Thomas and Martha enjoyed Sterne's Tristram Shandy early on, even reading it aloud to one another over those long evenings. As a result, we must see what becomes clearer as the story progresses: we are studying a man with no sense of humor.

A historic power struggle was brewing on the northern boundary of British North America as the youthful Jefferson grew to maturity and acquired the habits and lineaments of an educated gentleman. The Seven Years' War between Britain and France, known as the French and Indian War in American history books, foreshadowed the later Napoleonic struggle by taking place on many continents. British and French forces clashed in Europe, the high seas, India, and the Caribbean. They fought ferociously for Canada, particularly Quebec, using local tribes as surrogates and proxies. General James Wolfe's capture of the latter in late 1759 can be described as a watershed moment in history: it determined that English would be the future world language, and it indirectly precipitated the American Revolution, which caused the British Empire to establish Australia as an alternative destination for convicts and disgruntled laborers.

An enormous debate erupted in London about the future of triumphant British policy. The Indian subcontinent had been permanently wrested from France, and the Treaty of Paris in 1763 would allow Britain to assume leadership of at least one more French property. Guadeloupe or Canada were the only options. One party advocated for the claims of Guadeloupe, an island rich in sugar, spices, and slaves, the inclusion of which would nearly complete British domination of the Caribbean basin. Another side advocated for the acquisition of Canada, citing its enormous land for settlement, prospective abundance in furs, lumber, and minerals, and a large future market for British manufactured goods. In many ways, the second case—more forward-thinking and commercial—appeared to be the stronger and more persuasive one. It did, however, have an overlooked defect. If the British Crown acquired ownership of Canada, the thirteen American colonies would no longer be reliant on London's military protection against France.

William Burke had extraordinary foresight. Canada was conquered by the British. They also chose to raise taxes on their ostensibly grateful American subjects in order to recoup the high costs of the Seven Years' War, which had been fought in part to safeguard the thirteen colonies. This sparked a rebellion and, ultimately, political separation in 1776, with a France seeking vengeance for the humiliation of 1763 tipping the military balance against Britain. Many historians believe that the cost of this expedition to the impoverished French coffers exacerbated the financial crisis that forced King Louis to summon the Estates General and begin the disintegration of the ancien régime that culminated in the revolution of 1789.

Thus, Burke's theory foreshadows practically the entirety of Jefferson's long political career. An independent America was possible, first by skillfully manipulating rivalries between the two former major colonial powers, France and Britain, and then by playing a long hand with the ramshackle empire that had first conquered the Americas: the once-magnificent but now rapidly declining Spain. However, it should not be forgotten that America had fewer than five million people (almost one-fifth of them were African slaves), whereas France had twenty-seven million and Britain possibly fifteen million. As a result, the new republic was always forced to turn to the vast interior, on the rim of which it was perched. Jefferson was to emerge as the republican version of a philosopher monarch, coldly willing to sacrifice all convictions and allegiances for the single grand goal of making America permanent.

It took some time for Jefferson's life to catch up to the same tempo and rhythm that these simultaneous occurrences would require. He had become a member of Virginia's House of Burgesses in 1768, at the age of twenty-five, a part-time local parliament made of largely of his own class, and without much exhausting labor in the matter of election. Nonetheless, Jefferson took his responsibilities seriously and embarked—literally—on a project that appears to demonstrate how early the pattern of his life was set. He set out in a boat to investigate why the Rivanna River could not be navigable. Later, after identifying the impediments and determining that they were surmountable, he launched a plan for the clearing of the waterway, reducing the onerousness with which tobacco and other crops had previously been brought by land to the bigger but more distant James.

His father-in-law, John Wayles, died the same year. He gave to his daughter (which meant to his son-in-law at the moment) an estate that more than doubled Jefferson's ownership. He also left slaves to cultivate the land, including an illegitimate child of his, Sally Hemings, who became Martha Jefferson's half sister. Meanwhile, the young Jeffersons were having their own children, just two out of six of whom would survive infancy. The acquisition of this new fortune in real land and human property would plague Jefferson for the rest of his life, in fundamentally different ways, because it carried with it more debts and responsibilities than he was capable of managing. Still, he could have congratulated himself at the moment on having a nice house, a growing family, the respect of his colleagues, and the possibility of professional advancement.

In another era, he might have become famous regionally as an autodidact and innovator, earning a bucolic image as a severe but kindly slave-master and celebrated for the generosity of his table, the quality of his wines, and the breadth of his library and discussion. But something in him clearly generated irritation and drove him to seek a wider compass for his energy. Indeed, the British Empire's crises in North America made it difficult for everyone but the most obtuse to be content with a strictly private life.

However, in 1773, Jefferson was still able to maintain a balance between his private life and his official responsibilities. He was also able to envision a shaky balance between the political demands of Virginia in particular, the thirteen colonies in general, and the continuation of Crown control in North America. The normally placid House of Burgesses in Virginia had been dissolved by the British governor in May 1769 as a result of its insubordination in the matter of taxes, but the members, including Jefferson, strolled coolly down the street to the Apollo Room of the Raleigh Tavern—scene of his rebellion. However, in 1773, Jefferson was still able to maintain a balance between his private life and his official responsibilities. He was also able to envision a shaky balance between the political demands of Virginia in particular, the thirteen colonies in general, and the continuation of Crown control in North America. The normally placid House of Burgesses in Virginia had been dissolved by the British governor in May 1769 as a result of its insubordination in the matter of taxes, but the members, including Jefferson, strolled coolly down the street to the Apollo Room of the Raleigh Tavern— scene of his rejection on the dance floor by the maddening Miss Burwell—and there reconstituted themselves as a "Association" pledged to b (A monograph on the role of the bar in the American Revolution should be produced.) By modern standards, this was all good fun, and the insurrection died down within a year. However, it is relevant for our purposes for two reasons. The first is that the testy but deft governor, Norborne Berkeley, Baron de Botetourt, was a perfect embodiment of that "Norman yoke" on ancient English liberty that Paine, Jefferson, and others were beginning to resurrect as a propaganda item. The second reason is that the concept of economic warfare—of sanctions, boycotts, and embargoes—had taken root in Jefferson's open mind.

A Summary View demonstrates that Jefferson was a loss to the law and the bar, and that a client seeking an attorney who could plead on both sides of a matter would have been wise to hire him. Strangely, for someone who was about to be lauded for declaring universal ideas, Jefferson's core thesis was based on an essentially tribal appeal. He claimed that the original Saxon inhabitants in England had willingly relocated from the European continent to an island. And the North American immigrants had willingly relocated themselves from that island to another continent. Both had self-governing and autonomous communities. There was no loss of rights in either case: the Saxon's inborn and inherent freedom could not have been forfeited to King George any more than it could have been forfeited to the preceding Saxons of Germany. Rather, any Englishman anywhere in the world has the same rights as an Englishman in England. From there, it was simple to show that the King and Parliament judged the same individuals using different criteria: banning commerce, levying taxes, and extending the jurisdiction of distant courts only to the American branch. Jefferson made a scathing remark regarding the effect of this on the unjustly fined residents of Boston, saying that they were now delivered up "to ruin, by that unseen hand which governs the momentous affairs of this great empire." Adam Smith's Wealth of Nations, a defense of free enterprise that, incidentally, contended that colonies were a waste of resources, was not published until 1776. Maybe he saw a stray copy of A Summary View before suggesting his "invisible hand"?

However, in 1774, Jefferson and the majority of his companions considered it was still reasonable and prudent to clarify their differences with the Crown and to entreat the king to preserve the Anglo-Saxon family united under one imperial roof. "America was not conquered by William the Norman, nor were its lands surrendered to him or any of his successors."

However, between 1774 and 1776, American patriots had to rely only on their own right arms. There was natural reluctance to break with the mother country, but the arrogant king and his Tory ministers made the life of the waverer much easier by detecting the obviously seditious elements in Jefferson's suave Summary View and other similar and related protests, and acting as if a state of rebellion already existed. Local legislatures were disbanded, soldiers were disembarked, and "treason" proclamations were issued. Bitter conflicts erupted, primarily in Massachusetts. Loyalists and monarchists began to flee, either to Canada or to London. Paine's imperishable polemic became an instant best-seller in January 1776. By the summer, a Congress was convening in Philadelphia, and revolutionaries had a moral as well as a practical advantage in its debates. Jefferson made his way there, pausing only momentarily to attend to his unloved mother's obsequies.

His reputation as a resolution drafter, a writer of tremendous explanatory force, and a clever compromiser had preceded him. Indeed, Jefferson was nominated to the committee tasked with writing the Declaration in part as a result of a compromise. Richard Henry Lee, a Virginian, wrote the resolutions urging the thirteen colonies to declare independence, form a "confederation and perpetual union," and seek abroad recognition and military alliances. But he was needed back home, and Congress needed a Virginian just as much as it needed some New Englanders and middle-column representatives. The remaining members of the drafting committee were John Adams, Benjamin Franklin, Roger Sherman of Connecticut, and Robert Livingston of New York.

Several years passed before Jefferson was recognized as the Declaration's author, or until the words themselves "sunk in" and began to reverberate as they still do. As evidence of his amour propre, as well as his sense of history and rhetoric, he constantly hated the revisions made to his original by Congress. These are reproduced as parallel text in his own Autobiography, and have been scrutinized as thoroughly as the intellectual sources on which Jefferson relied when he retired to a modest boarding house for seventeen days, with only a Monticello slave named Robert Hemings—Sally's oldest full brother—at his disposal.

Indeed, Thomas Jefferson is one of only a few people whose name is associated with a sort of democracy. The term was not widely used at the time, and it was not always used positively. (John Adams had a habit of using the word "democratical" to signify "unsound" or "subversive.") However, the idea that government emerged from the people and was neither a gift or an imposition was perhaps the most radical aspect of the Declaration. Jefferson later compared governance to clothing as "the badge of lost innocence," reflecting on the Garden of Eden concept of primordial nakedness and guilt. Paine wrote in Common Sense, "Society is produced by our wants, and government by our wickedness." As a compromise between government as a necessary evil—or an unavoidable one—and as part of a bill of complaint against a hereditary monarch, the Declaration proposed the concept of "consent of the governed," launching the experiment known as American, or sometimes Jeffersonian, democracy.

The passage is unusually interesting. It demonstrates that Jefferson comprehended not just the horrors of chattel slavery on American soil, but also the horrible conditions of the Middle Passage between Africa and America, when so many lives were snuffed out callously. It also demonstrates, through the use of the word obtruded, that he knew how to appeal to his audience's sense of self-righteousness (how dare black men fight on the side of the British, as they frequently did?) and, looking further ahead, that he saw no future for free black people in America. The references to "piratical" and "infidel" show an early awareness of the Muslim slave racket carried on by the so-called Barbary kingdoms of Islamic North Africa: yet another dilemma that would play a role in Jefferson's subsequent career.

In retrospect, Jefferson had a tendency to conflate the subject of monarchy with the issue of slavery. In the Autobiography, he recalls his early days in the Virginia assembly after 1769, saying, "I made one effort in that body for the permission of slave emancipation, which was rejected: and indeed, nothing liberal could expect success during the regal government." The phrase "permission of emancipation of slaves," as lofty as it seemed, actually meant little more than a legal acknowledgement of individuals' power to "manumit," or liberate their "own" property. Even so, expecting us to think that, in the absence of the royal prerogative, a House of Burgesses comprised mostly of a club of tobacco farmers would cheerfully bestow liberty on their slaves is asking too much. Richard Bland, the member with whom Jefferson worked on this mild proposal, was labeled a "enemy of his country." (Note that he is not an adversary of his monarch.) One is compelled to suspect that the young guy was breaking a moral lance in a conflict he was certain of losing. And, with the benefit of hindsight, one might imagine that he despised the "obtrusion"—his proposed term in the Declaration—of a black population into Virginia in the first place, and subconsciously sought to blame a distant authority for this alien presence, or serpent, in the American Eden.

By September 1776, Jefferson felt he needed to return to Virginia, where he already had a seat in the legislature. So, after resigning from Congress, he came home and found himself entangled in another debate over first principles. In his absence, his own state had created its own Constitution, which Jefferson felt was necessary to fight due to its many entrenched conservative aspects. We can get a sense of how important this was to him since he received notification of his election by Congress to be a negotiator of a Treaty of Alliance between the United States and France in the month of his return to

Williamsburg, October 1776. This would need him to travel to Paris with Benjamin Franklin and Silas Deane. He expressed his disappointment in ways we were all too familiar with, citing the desire to spend more time with his family. This was not merely etiquette: he and his wife had already lost one child in infancy, and Martha herself was in poor health. Monticello's house and estate required attention. But Jefferson also wanted to establish himself in Virginia politics, which had been freed from royal influence.

Chapter 2:
War and Revolution in Virginia

At the Virginia level, the American Revolution was to be a true change of system rather than a change of master. These were land tenure, slavery, and state religious upkeep. The question of who would make the decision was superimposed: the people or the conventional authorities.

The earliest of these confrontations was over land reform. Jefferson despised the local legislation that preserved entail and primogeniture, or, to put it another way, the code of English feudalism, because of its Norman and anti-Saxon elements. This legislation stated that land might be held in perpetuity by families and that if an intestate landowner died, his holding would transfer wholly to his oldest son. After a lengthy debate that included a scuffle between his old instructor George Wythe and the more orthodox Edmund Pendleton, the Jeffersonian side prevailed, and both entail and primogeniture were eventually, albeit after many delaying tactics in committee, repealed.

Only the first eighteen words of this paragraph are inscribed in stone on the Jefferson Memorial in Washington, D.C., which was dedicated by Franklin Roosevelt on Jefferson's bicentennial in April 1943, during a period of optimism about human rights.

The statement grows more explicit as it continues, warning that if liberation and expatriation are not achieved peacefully, war will compel the same conclusions, and that "human nature must shudder at the prospect held up." We should not search for an example in Spain's deportation or erasure of the Moors. This precedent would be substantially too narrow in our instance." It offers some sense of the sick remorse and fear with which slaveholders saw the prospect of black vengeance, to the point that their most intelligent speaker could compare his chattels to a medieval Islamic army. And, but for the fact that this sanguinary euphemism is often omitted from the record, I hardly need to italicize the word deletion above. As a result, during Jefferson's tenure in Virginia politics, slave immigration was prohibited, and masters were given more leeway in freeing, or manumiting, their slaves. The urge to do so was one that Jefferson resisted, except for the children he had with Sally Hemings.

Jefferson went on to say that "our civil rights have no dependence on our religious opinions, any more than on our opinions in physics or geometry," and that religious tests for public office amounted to "bribing, with a monopoly of worldly honors and emoluments, those who will externally profess and conform to it; that though indeed these are criminal who do not withstand such temptation, so are those innocent who lay the bait in their way."

When the Jefferson-Madison arguments won out, the opposing side wanted to change the preamble by replacing the words Almighty God in the first line with the words Jesus Christ. Jefferson highlighted the amendment's failure by a large majority as "proof that they meant to comprehend, within the mantle of its protection, the Jew and the Gentile, the Christian and the Mahomedan, the Hindoo, and the Infidel of every denomination." Until 1776, the common-law punishment in Virginia for "heresy" was burning.

The Virginia Statute was enacted only one year before the Constitutional Convention in Philadelphia, and it had a significant impact on the omission of any mention of God from the resulting document, as well as the provision in Article 6, Section 3, that "no religious test" be required for the holding of any office. There were numerous different examples from which the Framers may have drawn, albeit they could not have used all of them. The Massachusetts Constitution of 1780 granted equal protection and the ability to hold public office only to Christians and only to Christians who rejected the pope. The New York Constitution of 1777 granted Jews equality but not Catholics. In Maryland, the situation was nearly the opposite, with rights granted to Catholics and Protestants but not to Jews, Deists, or freethinkers. Delaware forced its elected officials to swear to believe in the Trinity, while South Carolina made "Protestantism" its official religion. Virginia was the largest state in the new Union, and since so many of its sons were involved in the events of 1776, it possessed significant revolutionary prestige as well as weight. It is not totally outlandish to suggest that its

Statute on Religious Freedom was seminal in the First Amendment's "establishment" provision.

The second area in which Jefferson used Enlightenment theory as a policy tool was crime and punishment. He had been impressed by Cesare Beccaria's Dei delitti e delle pene (On Crimes and Punishments), published in Milan in 1764, and had copied no fewer than twenty-six portions from it into his 1776 Commonplace Book, as had many of his educated contemporaries. In his famous defense of the British soldiers wrongfully implicated during the Boston Massacre, John Adams quoted from Beccaria. Benjamin Franklin held high regard for Beccaria. Indeed, one of the major charges leveled by eighteenth-century radicals and liberals against the hereditary despotisms of the day was the monarchy's extensive use of torture and lethal punishment. Beccaria's treatise had shown the futility and idiocy, as well as the sadism, of these methods, which had been denounced as "cruel and unusual" in the words of the US Constitution's Eighth Amendment.

In 1778, Jefferson offered to the Virginia House of Delegates a "Bill of Proportion in Crimes and Punishments." He argued that Beccaria "had satisfied the reasonable world of the unrightfulness and inefficiency of the punishment of crimes by death." As an alternative, he proposed a plan of forced labor on public works. The measure was defeated by one vote, but it was passed in a weakened form in 1796.Despite his willingness to accept the inhuman practice of solitary confinement, which was later refined from Beccaria in the penal system proposed by Jeremy Bentham, Jefferson continued to press for a distinction between murder and manslaughter, which was recast as murder in the first and second degrees, and to evolve his interest in the "penitentiary" as a scientific matter, with graduated and appropriate punishments. Again, this cautious, calibrated liberalism was not to be extended to people of African origin.

Jefferson was 36 years old when he became Virginia's second governor, following Patrick Henry, who had served his maximum of three consecutive terms. The election was a pretty cordial and gentlemanly event, decided by Virginia's General Assembly, and Jefferson won by a slim margin against his buddy John Page.

Jefferson would have been happiest creating a new state capital in Richmond and allowing himself to pursue his architectural interests, but the state was still at war with the King of England, and this raw fact dominated his presidency. The capital was shifted from Williamsburg to Richmond, as Jefferson had planned, but only because it was closer to the sea and so less vulnerable to British attack. (Not that it was any less vulnerable, as Benedict Arnold demonstrated when he briefly seized the city in 1781.) Lord Cornwallis' redcoats reached Virginia, outmaneuvering the daring Marquis de Lafayette, and it wasn't long before Richmond was surrendered by the Continental army and the seat of government was moved to Charlottesville, Jefferson's hometown. His career, and perhaps his life, could have ended there if it hadn't been for the southern counterpart of Paul Revere's ride. When a smart Virginia cavalryman named Jack Jouett noticed a fast-moving column led by Lieutenant Colonel Banastre Tarleton heading toward Monticello, he drove his horse into a forty-mile nocturnal gallop to alert the Virginians that the British were coming, and coming quickly. Jefferson hardly had time to arrange the evacuation of the state government to Staunton before the invasion arrived on his doorstep. A number of his slaves took advantage of the opportunity to flee, maybe encouraged by cynical British promises of liberty, and this only added to their owner's shame.

Tarleton's attack occurred on the eve of May-June 1781, and Jefferson's stint as governor officially ended on June 2. Because the election of a successor had been delayed for ten days due to wartime necessity, Jefferson was only "acting" governor at the height of the crisis. Then, maybe overly concerned with legal form, he opted to rejoin his family. He no probably hoped to escape the suspicion of abdicating power in an emergency, but he was instead accused of something considerably more serious. He had, in effect, left his station in a dangerous situation. This may have meant less if Jefferson's governorship had not been a pretty hesitant affair all around, with Jefferson constantly balancing General Washington's need for more troops and his own unwillingness to impose conscription on free citizens. People are rarely at their best when they are terrified and defeated, and Jefferson's humiliation in 1781, which he blamed on himself, was to paint him with the coward's brush for the rest of his political career. This is despite his passionate, comprehensive, and effective defense of his own actions on the floor of the Virginia House following Cornwallis' loss and capitulation at Yorktown in October of that year. Everything may have been forgiven if Jefferson had just been governor for that final glorious event, but as it was, he was generally linked with the war's failures and retreats, and there is evidence that he never got over the bitterness of this. The contrast with Alexander Hamilton, who had served on Washington's staff with distinction and later led a brave assault at Yorktown, was especially vexing.

In his library, he opened the questionnaire sent to him by the French ambassador Francois Barbé-Marbois (future negotiator of the Louisiana purchase) in 1780. This document, which was also sent to the governors of the other American states, requested a detailed profile of Virginia. It was interested in learning about its natural history, resources, population, and laws. There could hardly have been a greater chance for Jefferson to demonstrate and prove his understanding. Though his Notes on the State of Virginia were not meant for publication at the time, and were not read by other eyes until several years later (sometimes in pirated and illtranslated form), today could be the time to revisit them.

Despite his intellectual curiosity, Jefferson lived at a time when the interior human eye, no matter how hard it tried, could not see as far as the horizon so soon to be mapped by Darwin. It was still a time of pseudo-science, nearly alchemy as opposed to chemistry. Jefferson was able to see through some of the period's quackeries, such as Mesmerism, but he was still a prisoner of knowledge's limitations, as well as one who sought a consistent explanation restlessly. Much of this is no longer relevant to us, but some of it was designed to cause long-term and irreversible harm.

Jefferson's method, on the other hand, was one of taxonomic minutiae. He caught and weighed various animals and ordered the excavation of a mammoth skeleton to demonstrate to Buffon that if size mattered, America was not deficient in natural vitality. (To his credit, and despite poetic passages in the Notes on Virginia's natural beauty, he never argued that America was superior in terms of scale or profusion.) But he never did figure out where the fossil shells came from.

More telling was Jefferson's candid assessment of the master-slave relationship's sexual character. "The whole commerce between master and slave is a perpetual exercise of the most boisterous passions, the most unrelenting despotism on the one hand, and degrading submission on the other," he said bluntly. The individual must be a prodigy to have his manners and morals intact under such conditions." He claimed that, even if blacks could not paint or write poetry in their natural form, they may improve on this lack of natural talent if given a transfusion of white blood. But he never felt that black poets or scientists, from Phillis Wheatley to Benjamin Banneker, could accomplish anything significant on their own or without the help of superior example.

Jefferson was still married to a white woman when he began writing the Notes. He became a widower in a relatively short period of time. Martha died in September 1782, cared to by Sally Hemings and others. Martha's death was precipitated in part by the birth of her sixth child, Lucy. As she was dying, she extracted a pledge from Jefferson that he would never marry again. It appears that her death completely prostrated him, yet it is also true that this disaster came just after a long series of failures and humiliations in the final months of his governorship. Perhaps this combination explains Monticello witnesses' descriptions of something resembling nervous weariness. But perhaps not, for he was soon able to return to the action.

Not long after his death, the Congress repeated his invitation to serve as an envoy abroad. He was asked to go to Paris alongside John Jay, John Adams, and Benjamin Franklin to help negotiate a deal with Britain. He accepted the offer, but after being delayed by ice-bound harbors on the east coast, he discovered that his services would not be required after all. The Treaty of Paris was signed faster than most people expected. The pact recognized the United States' independence, accepted American fishing rights up the coast of Canada, and conceded the region between the Alleghenies and the Mississippi. There was work to be done at home, and Jefferson was soon on his way to represent Virginia at the Confederation Congress.

After arriving and immediately getting down to business, he was essential in getting the Treaty ratified by a majority of the states (a fitting end to the effort initiated by the Declaration). He also contributed to the thrilling occasion of George Washington's resignation as commander in chief, a voluntary sacrifice of power that straightened every believer in republican virtue's shoulders and spines.

Expansion provided Jefferson with the opportunity to pursue his two main goals: Union enlargement and democratic expansion. Settlers began to pour across the Alleghenies, establishing chaotic land claims. Communities such as the Kentuckians, who were ruled by Virginia at the time, began to envision themselves as future states. Order was necessary, and Jefferson's intellect was anything but. He proposed that Kentucky become a self-governing state and prepared provisional maps for fourteen more using a strict latitudinal grid. This was done on purpose to anticipate, if not foreshadow, further western expansion—though it's probably a good thing that Jefferson's proposed state names (Cherronesus, Assenenisipia, and Metropotamia) were rejected. Rather than colonial government, the plan's essence was eventual voluntary membership to the Union. Anglo-Saxon traditions were once again put to use, with Jefferson proposing that each new region be split into "hundreds," with a hundred equaling ten square miles. He did not quite win this point, but the rectangular structure of American political geography bears his imprint (and it was also in this Congress that he saw his original proposal for a decimal dollar enacted). Under what became known as the Ordinance of 1784, adult male suffrage was to be the rule for the new states, and significant autonomy was granted in exchange for recognizing Congress' sovereignty and accepting joint responsibility for the federal debt. Jefferson, on the other hand, desired principle consistency. He stated that "after the year 1800 of the Christian era, there shall be neither slavery nor involuntary servitude."

Chapter 3:
Revolution in France

The posting in Paris did not start off well. Jefferson suffered another migraine attack and learnt of the child Lucy's death at Monticello, whose birth had hastened Martha's death. This terrible news, however, was delivered by a famous bearer—that of the Marquis de Lafayette, who was returning from a hero's tour in the United States. The Marquis was well connected and respected across Parisian society, and his relationship helped to ease unhappiness while also allowing access. Nonetheless, when questioned in renowned circles if he was Franklin's replacement, Jefferson was always cautious to emphasize that no one could replace the good Doctor—only surpass him.

America's standing in Europe was generally precarious. The British press, which was widely circulated, characterized the nascent republic as a savage and chaotic experiment that displayed all of the signs of failure. American commerce was shaky, and its military might was insignificant (hadn't France fought many of the battles for its independence?). Credit was difficult to obtain as a result of the massive debts created by Americans when they borrowed to support the revolution. Diplomatic representatives from the United States were forced to go to Amsterdam bankers and beg for loan extensions. Insults may be hurled with impunity, as Jefferson discovered to his chagrin while accompanying John Adams to London for a commercial treaty discussion. When the two men were presented before King George III at a reception in March 1786, they were treated with abhorrent harshness. The volatile monarch (who had actually treated Adams with civility on his initial appointment) did not appear to have forgiven or forgotten Jefferson's lese-majesté in the Summary View, let alone in the Declaration's phrasing. Jefferson's cautious retaliation for this oafish regal behavior, exacted in the White House many years later, would have significant ramifications of its own.

Because France had been such a stalwart ally against Britain during the Revolutionary War, and because Benjamin Franklin had been practically lionized at court as well as in French intellectual and scientific circles, America's attitude toward the French royal family was radically different. Nonetheless, Jefferson, who made frequent ventures outside of Paris, speaking to regular people whenever he could, was acutely aware that absolute monarchy was facing a reform, if not revolution, problem. His association with Lafayette introduced him to nobility—the Second Estate—who were willing to negotiate with the Third Estate, or disenfranchised people. (One can easily picture his attitude toward the First Estate—the Catholic Church, with its immense property holdings and religious monopoly, including official persecution of Protestants and Jews. We don't even have to imagine it. When Jefferson's daughter Patsy, who was enrolled in a convent school at the Abbaye Royale du Panthemont, wrote to him saying she wanted to become a Catholic and accept her vows as a nun, he drove directly to the school, retrieved her on the spot, and took her home.

The corruption and degeneration of the French social and economic order did not enrage Jefferson simply as a bystander. Almost all trade and commerce was in the hands of the so-called "FarmersGeneral," a state-backed cabal of propertied men who were "farmed out" the authority to levy taxes and imposts. One of Jefferson's responsibilities as minister was to open the French market to American products, particularly tobacco, in which he had a vested interest as a Virginia farmer. However, the Farmers-General retained control of the tobacco monopoly, and a series of arduous negotiations on this and other commodities contributed to Jefferson's conviction that the monarchical system was fundamentally flawed.

With his wife imprisoned in a nunnery, how likely was it that King Louis would act more prudently? Even after all discussions failed and the dramatic and stirring events of July 14, 1789, which Jefferson witnessed, he continued to identify with the Lafayette liberals, as it were. Despite holding a position of severe precariousness, of which they were mostly unaware, these liberals were rather revolutionary. The Marquis de Lafayette oversaw the destruction of the seized Bastille and gave its massive key to Thomas Paine as a special gift to George Washington. He then suggested to the National Assembly a "Declaration of the Rights of Man and of the Citizen," one of the modern world's foundation documents, in which Jefferson had some input. This sense of belonging to a vast and forward-thinking enterprise explains his indifference to the lynching and dismemberment of certain reactionary aristocracy, a price in blood he considered a minor one to pay in the circumstances. After all, hadn't the Assembly eliminated all feudal and clerical rights at once? Going beyond his official duties as a foreign minister, he hosted a dinner organized by the Lafayette faction in August, where a discussion ensued that he described as "truly worthy of being placed in parallel with the finest dialogues of antiquity, as handed to us by Xenophon, Plato, and Cicero." The committee agreed that the king should retain power, with an ultimate veto over legislation, but that the Assembly should function as a single body. With its separation of powers, this was hardly the spirit of Philadelphia. However, by the end of September 1789, Jefferson was safely aboard a ship and on his way home. It would only be a matter of time before Lafayette and his noble comrades were pushed into exile, and Thomas Paine was imprisoned in one of Maximilien Robespierre's jails. Perhaps paradoxically, Jefferson grew fonder of the French Revolution as it became more extreme: this was to provide a crucial inflection point in his political ascension.

Before we leave Paris, the subject of Sally Hemings must be addressed. Jefferson met her in Paris, where they began an affair that would last many years, generate many children, expose him to tremendous scandal—and confuse generations of American historians.

Sally Hemings was a white slaveholder's granddaughter and the daughter of another, John Wayles. Mr. Wayles was also the father of Thomas Jefferson's wife, Martha, making the wife and the latter mistress half sisters. To imply there was a taboo against "inter-racial" intercourse or "miscegenation" at Monticello would be greatly exaggerating. And, while she was undoubtedly a slave by virtue of being Jefferson's legal property, Sally—as I shall henceforth refer to her—had not been subjected to the humiliations and indignities of fieldwork or the lash. She had always been treated like a pampered housemaid. She was in the room when Martha Jefferson died, and she overheard Jefferson promise his dying wife that he would never marry again. She had clearly grown in at least two ways since then, and since Jefferson's departure for France. All stories describe her as extraordinarily beautiful (a photo would be wonderful), and Jefferson's relatives, Francis and Elizabeth Eppes, thought highly enough of her general moral and mental deportment to entrust her with a mission of some responsibility.

Professor Annette Gordon-Reed points out with well-controlled scorn in her brilliant, conclusive study of the subject, Thomas Jefferson and Sally Hemings: An American Controversy, that most analysts have refused to consider whether Sally had a mind of her own, or, even more shockingly, whether she made that mind up—in favor of an affair with a rich, famous, powerful, and fascinating man. We continue to deny or deny "agency," as modern parlance has it, to voiceless black female chattels. Unfortunately, Sally is still without a voice, and the single volume of Jefferson's letters that could have had correspondence with her is the only one in the entire large set that has gone missing. We don't even know if she was literate, which seems plausible, or if she spoke any French, which also seems possible. All we have is her son Madison Hemings' story that she obtained a commitment from Jefferson to liberate any children she had with him once they reached adulthood while in Paris. And the "only" evidence for that pledge is that he did, in fact, free them all, and no other slaves ever since.

Some historians believe that when they embarked for America, with Jefferson asking that she be berthed next to him on deck, Sally was pregnant, however the child, if there was one, did not live. However, all of her subsequent children, as recorded in Jefferson's "farm book" at Monticello, were born exactly nine months after one of his many visits to the residence. No other putative father was present at any of these times, which seems to put an end to the vile and unfounded idea, made by some famous historians, that Sally Hemings was giving or even selling herself to any male member of the Jefferson family. And the youngsters were all set free. In light of all of this, it was hardly necessary for the scientific journal Nature to publish in November 1996 a detailed DNA analysis, conducted by three laboratories in isolation from one another and unaware of the identities involved, that revealed an excellent match between blood drawn from Jefferson's and Hemings' descendants. Among other things, this precise genetic compatibility completely excluded Jefferson's nephews, Peter and Samuel Carr, on whom his white descendants, white society in general, and "damage-control" historians like Douglas Adair were willing to place any circumstantial blame or suspicion. Emerson observed that circumstances are often appealing as evidence, "as when you find a trout in the milk." But the evidence we now have, which is to fish and milk what cream is to coffee, and much more, leaves no room for reasonable doubt.

Chapter 4:
Interregnum

Jefferson's absence in France from 1785 to 1789 was extremely beneficial to his eventual political career. It earned him high marks as a diplomat and negotiator, but it also kept him out of, and to some extent above, the domestic fray. Both the Constitutional Convention in Philadelphia and Daniel Shays' revolt took place in his absence, giving him the ability to make comments without admitting blame. Most of his remarks were, in any case, private, as befitting a senior envoy, but this did not stop them from becoming widely known.

Shays' Rebellion, which was mainly a plebeian insurrection in Massachusetts against excessive taxation, also confronted the fledgling republic with the pressing issue of debt. This was caused by the British policy of pressing American merchants to pay their invoices in gold and silver. Daniel Shays, like William Jennings Bryan more than a century later, became the champion of all the ostensibly honest and hardworking farmers who perceived themselves oppressed by the implementation of a credit policy imposed by an urban elite. From 1786 to 1787, men and boys from numerous states rallied around Shays, who possessed the reputation of a former captain in George Washington's Continental Army. To put down the insurrection with the militia, Washington had to put forth a lot of effort.

There were two possible perspectives on Shays. One claimed that he embodied the original anti-tax, anti-authoritarian sentiments of 1776. The second was that he was a tyrant who threatened the very foundation of the new America. In Paris, Jefferson was firmly of the first opinion. "The spirit of resistance to government is so valuable on certain occasions, that I wish it to be always kept alive," he wrote to John Adams' wife, Abigail. It will frequently be used when it is incorrect, yet this is preferable than not using it at all. I enjoy a little defiance now and then. It's like there's a storm in the sky."
Jefferson had not yet heard of the slaughter that accompanied the uprising when he wrote this. But when he did get such news, he acted as if nothing had happened. "What signify a few lives lost in a generation or two?" he wrote to Adams' son-in-law William Smith. "The tree of liberty must be refreshed from time to time with the blood of patriots and tyrants." It is natural. Jefferson had not yet heard of the slaughter that accompanied the uprising when he wrote this. But when he did get such news, he acted as if nothing had happened. "What signify a few lives lost in a generation or two?" he wrote to Adams' son-in-law William Smith. "The tree of liberty must be refreshed from time to time with the blood of patriots and tyrants." It is its natural fertilizer." The keyword here must be "tyrants," not "patriots," because the only candidate for the latter title was the government to which Jefferson was acting as an envoy. Later chroniclers have noted Jefferson's occasional dismissive harshness when writing about the casualties suffered by individuals he approved of. This inclination, which is undoubtedly important for leadership, can always be expected to be quoted back at such a leader when he becomes the Establishment himself. (From Conor Cruise) O'Brien, the most venomous of Jefferson's adversaries, recalls how unafraid he was of repressing rebels he didn't like, such as slaves in Haiti. O'Brien also noted with dismay that Timothy McVeigh, when apprehended during the Oklahoma City massacre, was wearing a T-shirt that read, "The tree of liberty must be refreshed from time to time with the blood of patriots and tyrants." McVeigh's American fascist bomb was mostly built of fertilizer, which should give people who compare blood to manure pause.)

McVeigh is hardly the only subsequent figure who has resurrected Jefferson's words and used it against the all-powerful federal authority. However, the crucial element in 1786-87 was the absence of a central government. Shays, in fact, had just raised his standard against the Massachusetts state government before being defeated by presidentially authorized militia troops. A constitution that divided authorities and responsibilities between the states and the center was urgently needed. In the absence of the star of the previous Philadelphian show, a convention was convened in Philadelphia in 1787 to identify and produce such a document.

This veiled mockery concealed Jefferson's genuine conflicted feelings regarding the Constitution's worth. Would it weaken or strengthen the federal government? At first, he thought, and wrote to Adams, that the "strong" part was excessive, and that it had also been overdone and overwritten. "How do you feel about our new constitution?" I admit there are elements in it that make all of my dispositions dizzy." Returning to Shays, whose shadow had undoubtedly hung over the proceedings, he observed that "our Convention has been too much impressed by the insurrection of Massachusetts: and in the spur of the moment they are setting up a kite to keep the hen yard in order." With the seasoned tones of a veteran, he added that "all the good of it" might as well have been "couched in three or four new articles to be added to the good, old, and venerable fabric" of the Articles of Confederation (then only a few years old), which he described as being as worthy of preservation as "a religious relique."

Jefferson could not have anticipated that by arguing for a bill of rights, judicial scrutiny, and state autonomy and equality, he was laying the groundwork for his own future presidential campaign. However, he soon discovered that his varied proposals, no matter how discreetly intended, were being "leaked." In his absence, America had become far more politicized, despite the fact that the Constitution made little, if any, provision for political parties. In the short term, this made it more difficult for Jefferson to be on both sides of a debate (as when he expressed the hope that the Constitution would be ratified by a majority of states while also expressing the contrary hope that, in the absence of a bill of rights, some states would decline to ratify at all). In the long run, it prepared him for the more fractious politics inspired by the Federalism debate.

These inconsistencies in his own restless mind were well conveyed in a letter he wrote from Paris to James Madison in September 1789. It's debatable if it's crucial that he didn't mail the letter and didn't present it to Madison during their first encounter after his return from France, but he did finally send it to him in New York in January 1790. In it, he argued that "the earth should belong only to the living generation," and that they should possess it "in usufruct," with the same right as an independent nation to be free of the trammels of previous periods. He calculated a generation's life span to be nineteen years and advocated that all regimes, laws, and debts expire at such intervals, renewing humanity's lease on the earth's common purse. Adam Smith made a similar point, stating that "every successive generation of men have an equal right to the earth, and to all that it possesses," but Jefferson's exchange with Madison serves as a warm-up for the epic clash between Edmund Burke and Thomas Paine two years later. Paine declared in his Rights of Man that "man has no property in man," an assertion that may have worked well as an anti-slavery stance but instead condemned tradition and the hereditary principle as an enfranchisement of the dead over the living. Burke believed that society was a compact between those who had died, those who were still alive, and those yet to be born, and Madison anticipated him by admonishing Jefferson. Wasn't it true that previous generations built roads and bridges for the benefit of those who came after? Could it be true that generations passed over to their "successors" every nineteen years? Madison had already written a harsh critique of Jefferson's draft constitution for the state of Virginia, of his notion of the separation of powers, and of his view that disagreements over the separation should be addressed through direct appeals to the people in The Federalist, articles 47 to 51. This was more than just a difference in emphasis: it concealed diametrically opposing political ideologies.

There is no doubt that Jefferson was greatly affected in this by the French revolutionaries and their desire to remake the world. This was to be clearly expressed by their abandonment of the old calendar and their declaration of a new beginning for time. When Jefferson returned to the newly federalized United States, he took with him the conviction that the revolution of 1789 was a continuation and confirmation of the revolution of 1776, as well as the birth of a hardy ally for America against Britain's continuous intrigues. If George Washington had realized the full scope of this, he might not have extended Jefferson the invitation to become Secretary of State very immediately after his arrival.

Chapter 5:
Secretary of State

With his normal reluctance, Jefferson succumbed to Washington's appeal. He might have preferred reappointment to the office in Paris (who wouldn't, given the French Revolution's apparent pace and rhythm?). Alternatively, he could have prioritized his daughters' education and marriage, as well as the preservation of his Monticello estate. He was going to turn forty-six, which was quite elderly for the time. But he was fit and powerful, a widower, and a world traveler. He'd been bitten hard by the political bug while abroad, and it was clear to him that the future of American politics couldn't be left totally to his adversaries, even if they were friends.

This image was reinforced when he arrived at New York, the interim capital, in March 1790. Even before the Revolutionary War, the city had showed strong Tory tendencies, and now its salons seemed to reeks of an American pseudo-monarchism centered on a too-courtly President Washington. Jefferson did not suspect Washington of kingly aspirations (at least not at the time), but he was certain that a sycophantic retinue was striving to impose a system of rank and title. Before departing for Paris, he learnt through Madison that John Adams intended to address Washington as "His Highness, the President of the United States of America, and Protector of their Liberties," a form of salutation that he (Jefferson) derisively described as "superlatively ridiculous." To his relief, the House chose "Mr. President," but the threat was not over. After all, Adams was now vice president, and he could properly have hoped that any honor bestowed upon George Washington would subsequently be bestowed upon him, either by death or succession. It was an issue of fortifying Washington's democratic side while avoiding temptation from other directions.

Political factions did not have predictable names before then, however the phrases Federalist and anti-Federalist were widely used. When Jefferson attempted to characterize partisanship, he did so by nationalizing the issue and referring to elitists and would-be aristocrats as "Anglomanes" or other terms expressing nostalgia for the old country and its rule. In private and occasionally in public, he accepted the conclusion, which was the characterization of a decent American as a supporter of the French revolution.

His tenure as Secretary of State served as a good warm-up for his later years in office. The United States, still confined to the eastern seaboard, was confronted by the maneuverings of three superior powers—Britain, France, and Spain—all of which were operating on the same continent and dominating the high seas. To the west and inland, many Indian tribes were ready to form alliances with whoever appeared to be on the winning side. As the Shays' insurrection proved, there was a close link within the new state's political limits between the main domestic problem—that of indebtedness—and the vagaries of foreign policy. Jefferson's participation as a member of President Washington's inner circle, along with Alexander Hamilton, James Madison, Henry Knox, Edmund Randolph, and John Adams, was not limited to his own department of foreign relations.

The following battle could be described as triangular, however the triangle was far from equilateral. Abroad, it was vital to strike a balance between the three contending powers and capitalize on any disagreement between them. It was vital to avoid the supremacy of any one faction that was too closely connected with any foreign power at home. And on the border, keep an eye out for any opportunity to capture the Mississippi, without which the "United States" could only expect to be a coastal power with access to the vast interior. Jefferson approached this three-sided problem in the following manner. He fostered any signs of rivalry or jealousy among Britain, France, and Spain, while privately harboring a strong bias in favor of the French. He linked the British interest, as well as its domestic conservative equivalent, to individuals like Hamilton who advocated strict budgetary discipline. And he scoured the frontier for any hint of an opportunity, depending in the end on his strong counter-Malthusian assumption that Americans could outbreed all their enemies and replace any void with hardy new settlers without depleting food or other resources.

Alexander Hamilton quickly realized that his debt-reduction plan was facing a near-insurmountable populist backlash. It amounted to a tax on poorer people in poorer (mostly southern) states in exchange for a larger federal good that lay some time in the hypothetical future. The issue was stuck in Congress. It just so happened that it was also stuck on another. The Constitution required the establishment of a national capital city on ten square kilometers of territory. However, the place was not provided. One June evening in New York in 1790, Hamilton took Jefferson by the arm and beseechedly led him up and down Broadway toward the president's residence. Nothing less, he claimed, was at stake in the debt issue than the Union's very survival. This was not an easy argument to dismiss, and Jefferson agreed to organize a dinner the following evening with himself as the referee between Hamilton and his main legislative challenger, James Madison. At this dinner, it was decided that Hamilton would get as many votes in Congress as Jefferson and Madison could guarantee, and that the new capital of the country should be built on the Potomac, where Maryland and Virginia converged, to "sweeten the pill" for the southern states. This intended to happen after a ten-year construction period, during which Pennsylvania might be placated by having the nation's capital in Philadelphia.

The first round was handily won by Hamilton. The first of Edmund Burke's attacks on the French Revolution, made in early 1790 and consisting of a near-hysterical speech to the British Parliament on anarchy and madness in Paris, was chosen for publication by Fenno's Gazette. It appears that Jefferson wanted this publication as something that would undermine Burke as a zealous Tory. For the rest of the time, he dismissed any serious news from Paris as simple British propaganda, and he was able to "manage" the public's perception of unfolding French events by using the State Department's power to decide which periodicals printed federal statutes. However, Alexander Hamilton recognized the importance of British trade and the British link, which was still very strong in the northern states, and made steps to guarantee that government advertising, a prerogative of his Treasury Department, was allotted advantageously to the Gazette. This prompted Fenno to change his editorial tone in late 1790 (and serves as a reminder that even our wigged and literate Founding Fathers were susceptible to vulgar politics).

The extent to which George Washington was aware of, or interested in, rivalries between his subordinates is debated by historians. (It is common to believe that he was above the battle or unaware of it.) In any case, once Benjamin Franklin died in April 1790, the president delegated the handling of the many rival tributes that poured to and from the National Assembly in Paris and the American Congress to Hamilton rather than Jefferson. The subtext of these flowery praises and statements of esteem was also a measure of French-American solidarity, and it appears clear that Washington did not want to give any hostages to fortune until he knew who he was dealing with in France. Jefferson may have surrendered to the inevitable in this case, and he may have loved the thought of an American conservative like Hamilton performing the obsequies for France's favorite American, but he did not abandon his role in the proxy battle between Burkeans and Paine-ites.

In May 1791, Thomas Jefferson and James Madison embarked on a journey that produced a rich vein of gossip at the time and, better still, has provided material for historians to speculate on ever since. Under the guise of a "botanizing tour," they departed their usual haunts in Virginia to collect specimens up and down the Hudson Valley and into western New England. Despite their keen interest in flora and animals, they devised a scheme to alternate interactions with nature with private meetings at the homes of local anti-Hamiltonians. They met Philip Freneau for breakfast in New York City and encouraged him in his anti-Federalist journalism. They appear to have been intrigued in Aaron Burr, whose populist campaign had deposed the "aristocratic" Dutchman Philip Schuyler, Hamilton's father-in-law, as New York senator. Jefferson and Madison did not meet Governor George Clinton, who was emerging as an early model of the big-city political boss at the time. But they were planning, if not rehearsing, a coalition of southern and northern anti-Federalists against England's despised party. Jefferson and Madison returned to Virginia peacefully, where Madison would become Jefferson's surrogate voice anytime the later felt the need to remain on the tactical sidelines.

Hamilton's increasingly effective promotion of a National Bank, regulating debt, trade, and securities and based on the concept of stable commerce with London and an abhorrence of revolutionary excess in France, was a triumphant success for that "English party" in the meantime. When Washington asked Jefferson for his opinion, he claimed that the Constitution had no such provision. He was concerned about the rise of an unaccountable center of authority, one with an Anglomane demeanor. On this point, Hamilton argued effectively that the Constitution was subject to imaginative interpretation rather than rigid construction or "original intent," and that the section granting Congress all "necessary and proper" powers would suffice. Jefferson, whose attitude toward deficit financing was heavily influenced by his own crippling indebtedness as a Virginia planter, could never relinquish the notion that paper money and borrowing were immoral, as well as unstable and evil.

As a cat's-paw, he began to use a protégé of Madison's named William Branch Giles, a Virginia congressman with a slicing legislative manner. Giles suggested a series of resolutions demanding Hamilton to produce massive volumes of Treasury data as soon as feasible. The Virginians assumed Hamilton's fast movements of money and accounts must conceal something disgusting, but in every case, the Treasury secretary outperformed his detractors by providing factual statements within near impossible timeframes. Frustrated, Jefferson crafted a general vote of no confidence in Hamilton for his "maladministration," which he used to offer in the House through Giles. With its defeat, Hamilton's mercantile modernism rapidly overwhelmed his rural concept of fiscal honesty. Washington, and eventually Congress, supported not only the establishment of the bank, but also Hamilton's overall leadership.

The appointment of Gouverneur Morris as American envoy to France could be added to Jefferson's list of reversals. This crusty, peg-legged person was considered by Jefferson as "a highflying monarchy man," and as yet another manifestation of George Washington's conservatism on the French situation. But Jefferson decided to put all of his faith in the moral and political inspiration of the Parisian revolution, which he thought would spread throughout the world and derail all conservatives' well-laid schemes, both foreign and domestic. This conviction drove him to make several rash decisions that he later regretted.

However, it must have appeared to Jefferson in early 1793 that he had, after all, supported the right horse. The army of revolutionary France successfully defeated an invading alliance of panicked European monarchs, promising in hushed tones to export world revolution on republican bayonets. American public opinion was fervently, even ecstatically, pro-French. The execution of King Louis in February was largely regarded as nothing more than natural justice, similar to that applied to England's King Charles I. Most importantly, the US was not alone: it had a powerful and great ally. But there was a little chiaroscuro missing from this wonderful image. The more the revolution spread in Paris, the more America's old pals in the city seemed to lose their eminence, liberty, or even their heads. In his generally counterrevolutionary reports to the State Department, Gouverneur Morris was cold and cynical on this point, and there were those among American conservatives who thought that, whatever the comparison with King Charles I, Jefferson was privately studying (as John Adams put it) for the role of a future American Cromwell.

This moment of Jeffersonian ecstasy would not last long. For one example, after decapitating the monarch of France, the French revolutionaries declared war on the king of England. The humiliation of a new French envoy, hotfoot from the new regime in Paris and foolishly convinced that America was a place where his welcome could never be worn out, was added to the worrisome matter of the correct American response to the onset of war. This was Edmond Charles Genet, a guy whose arrival on the scene was a great combination of tragedy and farce, both of which were ultimately at Jefferson's expense.

This is how things stood, or had been, until 1793. The United States had an alliance pact with France dating back to 1778, which served as the seal of Franco-American brotherhood throughout the Revolutionary War. It also had a trade treaty with France dating back to 1786, which stated that in the event of war, French belligerent vessels would be given preferential treatment in American ports. However, the US was constantly negotiating with Britain to normalize commercial and military relations, as well as to put an end to the British practice of impressing or kidnapping sailors off American ships. Hamilton and the other English friends contended that the treaties with France were no longer valid because they were signed with the previous monarchical state. Washington bridged the gap by releasing a "Proclamation" declaring the United States "impartial" (rather than "neutral," as Hamilton had desired). Jefferson desired two things: for America to profit from any Anglo-French war, at the very least by providing both sides with "necessaries," and for England to be crushed by the global growth of French "republicanism." (Around this time, persons in America who identified as "republican" were forming "Democratic" societies and clubs, with Jefferson serving as their unacknowledged patron.) As a result, his duties as Secretary of State were in direct conflict with his domestic political ambitions. He might have handled the paradox better if it hadn't been for Citizen Genet.

This showy and obnoxious guy arrived in Charleston in May 1793, shortly after George Washington issued his wise Proclamation. Not impressed by such a compromised gesture, Genet accepted a series of celebratory parties, banquets, and parades, adorned with his own florid toasts and speeches, all the way across the country to Philadelphia. It has been speculated that Jefferson did little to discourage this Francophile demonstration. But he must have started to regret it almost as soon as Genet handed his credentials to President Washington, who had kept paintings of King Louis and Marie Antoinette on the wall of his Philadelphia home.

Jefferson's following few months were a nightmare. He longed to join in the public popularity generated by Genet's arrival, but his own personal reticence, as well as his well-honed diplomatic skills, kept him away from Genet's vulgar excesses. It was clear that the new French ambassador regarded Americans' "impartiality" as a polite fiction, was willing to infiltrate anyone in order to gain immediate access to American harbors for French warships, prize ships, and privateers, and was not above appealing to voters over the heads of the administration. His fatal tactlessness was not limited to the

Atlantic theater. With Spain's relationship with Britain reestablished, Genet intended to trouble the borders of Spanish-held Louisiana with landhungry Kentucky adventurers. Jefferson allowed himself to make a significant misstep here. Advised in advance by Genet, who embarrassingly took him into confidence "not as Secretary of State, but as Mr. Jefferson," he stated that he could not bear the use of Kentuckians against Spanish territory, but that, putting this consideration aside, he "did not care what insurrections should be excited in Louisiana." He undoubtedly allowed his ambition for westward expansion and aggravation with the stalling negotiations with Spain regarding Mississippi navigation get the best of him here. He was also apprehended when the Spanish authorities discovered the involvement of some of his associates in border subversion, and was then forced to issue orders prohibiting any such activity, couched with a sternness that he did not personally feel.

Genet finally went too far in early July 1793, just in time for the American Independence Day celebrations. He insisted on refitting and relaunching a British warship seized by the French as a privateer, and he did not wait for an answer. The Hamilton faction would have preferred that the ship—annoyingly renamed La Petite Démocrate—be fired upon before setting sail under its new flag, and President Washington was almost equally enraged; even more so when it was discovered that the privateer had left anchor before any decisive action could be taken. Instead, vengeance was exacted on the French minister, whose appointment Jefferson now saw as "calamitous." He promised to compose a lengthy letter seeking Genet's recall to Paris. The reaction to this diplomatic maneuver was another evidence of how things were going in Paris. Despite his revolutionary rhetoric, Genet had been a member of the Girondin group and was unpopular with the regnant Jacobins. Those in power would have been perfectly content not only to recall him, but also to hang him. Genet eventually chose to remain in America, where he married the daughter of New York Governor George Clinton and, staying at least a Jeffersonian, pursued the calm pursuit of agriculture.

The overall dishonor imposed on the prestige of the French Revolution was a personal embarrassment to Jefferson. He had done everything he could to limit the damage. The cabinet voted to publish the records related to the affair in the face of a massive public uproar against Genet's depredations. Jefferson, whose job it was as secretary of state to oversee this, was able to slip in some similarly devastating information regarding British naval threats to American trade. Thus, he narrowly avoided the general wreckage of the French group, and even managed to seem as someone who could submit his own inclinations to the needs of his country. As a fitting end to his tenure as Secretary of Commerce, he delivered to Congress a lengthy and brilliant "Report on American Commerce." In this document, he proposed an America committed to international free trade, unattached to any nation, and willing to use economic rather than military force. The report, which borrowed heavily from Adam Smith's Wealth of Nations, was also intended to be an alternative to Alexander Hamilton's pro-British mercantilism.

This tenacity, far exceeding what became known in American politics as a "Sherman declaration," may have persuaded George Washington, who had urged him not to resign sooner and had in fact postponed his own resignation as part of the bargain that kept him on, but it did not impress men like John Adams, who were already sick of Jefferson and his striking of sensitive and superior attitudes. It's possible that Jefferson meant it this time because his time as secretary of state had been deeply wounding and frustrating, and because his final months in office were overshadowed by a dreadful outbreak of yellow fever in Philadelphia, which poisoned local existence and nearly paralyzed the government. Albemarle County's cold mountains must have beckoned like never before. Nonetheless, he must have been acutely aware that he had left America in deadlock, as between Federalists and Republicans, England and France, and the putative heirs of the elderly George Washington.

Thus, Jefferson's heart is broken not merely for a slaveholding caste, but also for their fate as a tragedy without precedent. He is pleading with his fellow Virginian to secure public funds to assist and sustain these exiles from the principles of 1789. (Perhaps not in 1789; the French regime would not technically abolish slavery until the next year, 1794, although slavery had been eradicated in Haiti by then.) Jefferson apparently believes that such compassion will soothe French sentiment after the battering it has endured at the hands of

Americans, and it is worth noting that this letter to Monroe is issued in the same month that "Citizen" Genet is finally disowned—by Jefferson himself.

It is also worth noting that Genet, like many of his fellow Girondins, was a member of the Parisian political club known as Les Amis des Noirs, and that Jefferson was contacted to endorse this organization prior to 1789 but declined. During his stint as envoy to America, Genet's anti-slavery beliefs were utilized to discredit him among southerners. that a result, Jefferson held the same opinion of Haiti that he did of Virginia: abolition could be as destructive and immoral as slavery itself. Because of this bias, he did not recognize at first that events in Haiti would one day give him with a historic opportunity.

Chapter 6:
In Waiting

Jefferson, who had been in retreat at Monticello since the beginning of 1794, may have meant to remain there. In the fall of that year, he very definitely turned down an offer from Edmund Randolph, his successor as Secretary of State. Randolph wanted him to be the negotiator for a new treaty with Spain. Jefferson not only declined the offer, but also stated that no incentive of any type could entice him back into politics. However, it may be argued that he was conserving himself for something more favorable.

During these years, he retrenched and updated his famous residence due to financial constraints. He remained an agrarian, as seen by his newly constructed plow, which was based on an earth-cutting technique he initially saw in France, and his acquisition of a more effective threshing machine from Scotland. He made some concessions to industrialism by constructing a nail-making factory on the estate and forming a primitive manufacturing line with the younger male slaves. A vast replica of the Palladian mansion was undertaken, with some of its innovations (the dumbwaiter, the revolving entrance, the views from the windows) positioned in such a way as to minimize any direct contact with the slaves themselves.

Jefferson, who had reached the age of fifty while serving as Secretary of State, became a grandfather with the birth of Martha's children to Thomas Mann Randolph. In 1795, he became a father for the second time, with the birth of Sally Hemings' first reported child. He remained mentally and physically youthful and hale for his age, and he exercised regularly on horseback and with his trusty pistol. How likely is it that he could have avoided the political imperative for long? Only if members of his own political faction had the upper hand in the nation's affairs. However, by the end of 1794, the news (and his own correspondents) informed him that this was not the case. In western Pennsylvania, an insurrection known as the Whiskey Rebellion erupted in response to a federal excise on liquor distilling. The political leadership of this movement, which was inspired by the French Revolution, advocated calling itself a "Committee of Public Safety" following Jacobin lines at one point. George Washington, Alexander Hamilton, John Adams, and John Jay, for their parts, were quick to spot the subversive hand of the newly founded, Republican-leaning "Democratic Societies." They dubbed these "self-created societies," as if there were any other kind. The militia was summoned from numerous neighboring states, and a force of fifteen thousand soldiers, led by Hamilton, was sent into battle against the radicals. This display of overwhelming authority had the effect of quickly defeating the uprising.

It was also enough to enrage Jefferson. In a letter to Republican leader in Congress James Madison, he described the president's speech as "an attack on the freedom of discussion, the freedom of writing, printing, and publishing." He returned to the concept of a perpetual struggle between liberty and tyranny, as he had done with the example of the Shays' Rebellion. The administration was "monarchical," with a mindset that was "perfectly dazzled by the glittering of crowns and coronets." Exaggerating slightly, he believed he observed a propensity to separatist among the rebels, which, if dealt too harshly, would endanger the Union.

On the same day that Washington launched his attack on "self-created" communities, Chief Justice John Jay signed a pact in London. When the contents of the agreement with Britain were revealed, a massive nationalistic and populist reaction erupted. The British agreed to withdraw from their positions in the American Northwest, which was little more than what they had promised in 1783. Americans were to be permitted to trade freely with the British East Indies, but not with the nearby West Indies. Competing claims for losses in previous wars were settled, albeit mostly in favor of British creditors. Above all, and clearly understood by public opinion, the British refused to make any commitment on their widely reviled impressments, or virtual kidnappings, of American mariners.

If Jefferson is going to London to celebrate the reawakenings of 1776 and 1789, why not go as far as Philadelphia? Several months later, when Republicans in Congress failed miserably in their bid to defeat the Jay Treaty, his tone softened. Then, on September 19, 1796, the "Farewell Address" of President George Washington was published, which everyone expected but no one had properly prepared for. To all Republicans, there was an immediate sense of a vacuum, both in national authority and in their personal leadership.

Jefferson was well aware that Vice President John Adams would be the likely winner in any election to succeed Washington, and he may have wanted (as he stated) this outcome. There was something to be said for avoiding any direct comparison to the Father of the Country, as well as avoiding the allegation of vaulting ambition. The party, however, would not be denied, and after informing Jefferson that he would not be running, James Madison organized with the Republican leadership for a caucus to simply designate Thomas Jefferson and Aaron Burr as the candidates. On what may be called this assumption, the election proceeded in a stately manner. Reflecting on the election of Jefferson and Adams in 1796, the electors were given a choice between the president of the American Philosophical

Society and the founder of the American Academy of Arts and Sciences, and they picked both.

After Washington left, American politics became more overtly partisan. At first, both Adams and Jefferson worked hard to keep their politics in check. Jefferson opted not to send Adams a congratulatory letter in which he chastised Alexander Hamilton. Adams kindly suggested that Jefferson head a high-level trip to France to appease Parisian outrage over the John Jay pact with England. (The new vice president turned down the honor, preferring to head the Senate and subsequently write a small, exquisite book on order and process that is still in use.) Both men were inaugurated in a cordial manner. But none of this could erase the distrust that the two men had for each other, which had existed since the Burke-Paine controversy in 1791, or the fact that they saw Anglo-French rivalry, and its domestic analogues, from diametrically opposing views.

Jefferson believed that those who yelled the loudest about "foreign influence" were the primary agents of it. He never got over the suspicion that Hamilton was plotting a pro-British coup. As Senate President, he was frequently subjected to the most venomous insults, both of himself and of competing factions by one another. He made a noteworthy remark about one such squabble, in which a Connecticut Federalist and a Vermont Republican went from insults to violence. "These proceedings," he remarked sarcastically, "must degrade the General Government and lead the people to lean more on their state governments, which have sunk under the former's early popularity."

Without pausing to consider the blatant nature of that last provision, Vice President Thomas Jefferson initially took a position on two points. First, he believed the measures were aimed squarely at foreign radicals and dissidents who had previously considered the United States to be their second home. He envisioned men like the French philosophe Constantin Volney, whose anticlerical masterpiece The Ruins he had assisted in translating, or the Polish hero Thaddeus Kosciusko, volunteer commander in the American Revolutionary War. Both men felt driven to depart from the land that had honored them with their presence. Second, he saw the regulations governing publication and advocacy as a direct violation of the First Amendment to the United States Constitution, and hence as outside the purview of Congress. The Federalists made a minor compromise by amending the proposed law to exclude "prior restraint" of publishing, but they passed it triumphantly on Bastille Day 1798, and they enforced it with some vigor against Republican editors and pamphleteers.

For the second time, Jefferson may have felt a smidgeon of independence as a result of his absence in Paris at the Constitutional Convention. He represented a middle ground between orthodox, dogmatic anti-Federalism and the more spontaneous form. He collaborated with James Madison to draft resolutions from two states that repealed the Alien and Sedition Acts. I say "negating" because the two resolutions differ just little yet profoundly. The Kentucky version, created by Jefferson himself, effectively "nullified" federal law as it applied inside the confines of that state. Scholars of constitutional law utilize the Virginia resolution, which is more influenced by Madison, to explain the doctrine of "interposition." According to this interpretation, a state may hide its inhabitants from federal judgements and invite other states to assess the legality and justice of the situation. (Despite this nicety and delicacy, Alexander Hamilton, who had risen to prominence as a military figure in the Adams administration, proposed dispatching federal troops to Virginia to demonstrate who was in authority.)

Within two years, Jefferson had been arraigned as an abolitionist by pro-slavery forces and had provided the moral rhetoric of states' rights that was to become the major political prop of the pro-slavery movement. During the same row, he was to give his opponents a lash that he would feel throughout his lifetime. James Callender, the genius of scurrility, was one of the Republican journalists caught in the web of the Sedition Act. This exiled Scottish son wrote so vehemently against President Adams and Alexander Hamilton that he was tried and subsequently imprisoned.

Jefferson, noticing the man's talent and sympathizing with his position, made discreet financial contributions to him and took him into confidence as a man who might one day be useful. He therefore began a career that would culminate in the first gruesome exposé of his personal affair with Sally Hemings.

The potential clash between state rights and High Federalism was never openly debated or confronted. Two simultaneous occurrences supervened due to the coincidences that give accident its necessary role in the recounting of history. The first of these was the full takeover of power by the Corsican usurper Napoleon Bonaparte in France. After establishing himself as "First Consul" on 18 Brumaire 1799, the new military ruler wasted no time in declaring that the French revolution had come to an end after ten turbulent years. On December 15, 1799, this "Proclamation" was issued. George Washington had died the day before. No two events, alone or together, could have given Americans a clearer sense of the coming new century.

If Washington's departure as president had shown profound splits between contending groups, his death would reveal deep divisions inside his own Federalism party. And the most important of these divisions concerns relations with France. Dr. George Logan, a well-meaning Quaker, had gone to Paris to see if the "quasi-war" could not be replaced by a peace. (His name lives on in today's Logan Act, which was enacted by irascible Federalists to prohibit unaccredited American citizens from engaging in private diplomacy.) He returned with reasonable evidence that there was goodwill on the French side, if only because of Admiral Horatio Nelson's crushing defeat of the French navy at the mouth of the Nile by the rear guard of Bonaparte's Egyptian expedition. Jefferson was caught off guard by events. President Adams was well aware that his additional taxes for a larger military apparatus had proved unpopular, at least in the absence of a full-fledged war with France. Hamilton recognized this rationale, yet he demanded a war. Adams bought time by dispatching a new team of negotiators to Paris. Meanwhile, with the arrival of an imperialist Napoleon, Jefferson felt free to abandon any allegiance to the revolutionary or republican French. (In this, he may have unintentionally imitated his despised Federalist adversaries, who contended that treaties established with King Louis were null and void once the monarchy was destroyed by the Jacobins.)

Professor Garry Wills has added a grave charge to this head-swimming collision of arithmetic and interest (not really cleared up until the passage of the Twelfth Amendment to the Constitution in 1804, and still a possible anomaly to this day, should there be any question of the validity of any state's ballot). According to this narrative, Jefferson's vote was considerably inflated by ballots cast on behalf of disenfranchised slaves in the south, who were counted as "three fifths" of a citizen under the federal Constitution and had the same weight in the Electoral College. The "three fifths law" did not apply to the Senate, and Professor Wills' enthusiasm for Pinckney may still be justified by Jefferson's indebtedness to "the slave power" and his awareness of that indebtedness. Nonetheless, it might be stated that it casts a shadow over 1801 as a "second revolution," or a new beginning for democratic politics.

In reality, the sight in the House in February 1801 was less than inspiring. Many, if not most, Republicans had mistakenly concluded that Burr was just running for vice president, and many had voted for him as a manner of atoning for his poor showing (particularly in the South) in 1796. Burr, on the other hand, has an unusual blend of characteristics. He was the grandson of the fiery Calvinist preacher Jonathan Edwards, and he was a hero in the bedroom and boardroom as well, with many rich speculations to his credit. He had the ability to make lifelong friends and adversaries. Alexander Hamilton, a fellow New Yorker and future victim, was one of his more persistent adversaries. Indeed, Hamilton, to his credit, swallowed his hatred for Jefferson in his hatred for Burr. A lot of prominent Federalists agreed with Hamilton that Burr's election would be a disaster. After thirty-five stalemate ballots in the House, the tie was eventually broken on the initiative of Delaware's James Bayard. His state, along with South Carolina, abstained from voting for Burr, while Vermont and Maryland abstained. On February 17, 1801, Thomas Jefferson was elected as the third President of the United States on the 36th ballot.

Another significant point in Jefferson's address was his assertion that, while America would seek friendly relations with all nations, it would enter into "entangling alliances with none." This was his clandestine farewell to the French, as well as an indication of his ambition for the United States to become an independent power. A new capital city in Washington, a new century, a new president, and—who knows?—maybe even a new epoch.

Chapter 7:
Mr. President

According to historian Robert Davis, between 1530 and 1780, Muslim autocracies on Africa's northwest coast kidnapped and enslaved as many as a million and a quarter Europeans. This trade, which combined piracy, ransom, and enslavement, was not on par with the infamous Middle Passage, in which so many bartered black Africans died, nor was it as organized and commercialized as the "triangular" slave trade that flourished between Europe, Africa, and the Americas. It did, however, originate in some ways from that trade, given that European invaders had disrupted an earlier North African Arab engagement in a north-south trafficking of African slaves. Many credible period chronicles describe "Barbary" raids on coastal cities as far away as England and Ireland, as well as numerous abductions from and of boats in the Mediterranean and other seaways. In 1631, for example, it appears that nearly every resident of the Irish town of Baltimore was taken away. Both Samuel Pepys and Daniel Defoe mention the slave trade in their works, with Robinson Crusoe himself spending some time as a captured slave. With the Barbary fear in mind, James Thomson's renowned 1740 popular song "Rule Britannia," with its chorus about Britons "never, never, never" being slaves, was penned.

It was European countries' general policy to establish separate peace treaties with the rulers of Algiers, Morocco, Tripoli, and Tunis (and it had also been some of them's policy to acquire Muslim slaves when they could, as well as to vary the business with an occasional punitive expedition). By the time of the American Revolution, however, most European capitals had agreed to pay a set amount of tribute to the "Barbary" powers—so-called partly because of their original Berber population, but also because of the convenient euphony of the word with barbarism—in exchange for either redeemed captives or broader immunity from plunder and kidnapping. It was included in the cost of doing business. It might also be used to isolate a competitor nation in secret discussions with one or more emirs or sultans.

The new America could scarcely approach this with calm. It lacked a navy with which to protect its commercial ships or to threaten vengeance. Its trade had actually deteriorated as a result of losing such protection from the British Empire. Furthermore, furious factions in London were not above inciting North Africans to board American ships and thus give the seceding colonies a lesson.

During his service as the United States minister to Paris and London, respectively, Thomas Jefferson developed a strong dislike for the situation. The American ship Betsey, with a crew of ten, was captured by a Moroccan corsair in 1784 while travelling from Cádiz, in southern Spain, to Philadelphia with a cargo of salt. Algerian ships grabbed the Dauphin and the Maria in the Atlantic not long after. Secretary of State John Jay had urged his two American envoys in New York to follow the European precedent and sign treaties with the abductors. They were given permission to borrow significant sums of money from Dutch financiers in order to pay tribute.

It is difficult to imagine a better summary of everything Jefferson despised about monarchy and religion, but he did not dwell on it, preferring to advise the administration to refuse all payment of tribute and to prepare immediately to outfit an American naval squadron to visit the Mediterranean. In the long run, he wrote, a worldwide concert of powers comprised of all nations whose shipping was being targeted by predatory raids was required. "Justice and Honor favor this course," he said, adding that it would also save money in the long run.

John Adams did not share this viewpoint. He agreed that "Avarice and Fear are the only agents at Algiers," and that "it would be a good occasion to begin a navy," but he was certain that Congress would never allocate the funds for a punitive mission, and the US had no navy to speak of in the meanwhile. "Based on these premises, I conclude that it is best for us to negotiate and pay the required sum as soon as possible." Concerning the piratical Islamic nations, "we ought not to fight them at all unless we are determined to fight them forever." Jefferson's opinion of Adams, in my opinion, began to deteriorate at that moment. He did, however, make a ceremonial bow to the seeming wisdom of such a strategy as the junior.

In private, he had long since decided that there would be a reckoning with the Barbary corsairs. In the slave trade line that was cut from his first copy of the Declaration of Independence, he spoke caustically to the "Christian king of Great Britain" engaged in "this piratical warfare, the opprobrium of infidel powers." This appears to be a direct reference to Barbary practices. Long before the encounter with Abdrahaman, in November 1784, he wrote to James Madison, "We ought to begin a naval power, if we mean to carry on our own commerce." Can we start on a more honorable note or with a weaker foe? I believe [John] Paul Jones, with a half-dozen frigates, would completely crush their commerce." Later, while in Paris, he became acquainted with John Paul Jones, a maritime hero of the American Revolution who is often regarded as the creator of the United States Navy. Jefferson appears to have started the relationship by acting as a go-between for Jones and his then-current mistress, Madame Townsend. She was the widow of an Englishman and King Louis XV's rumored illegitimate daughter. We only know her identify through Jefferson's papers: he appears to have fulfilled his middleman job with considerable skill (another proof of his worldliness in matters sexual), but he appears to have stopped short of granting her a loan when she requested one. In late 1787, Jefferson presented a very different suggestion to Jones. He had learned through diplomatic channels that Russia's Empress Catherine ("the Great") would like to hire the naval hero as the commander of a fleet with the sole intention of driving the Turks out of the Black Sea.

Jones was in dire financial and emotional straits at the time and was tempted to take the job. But why was Jefferson making it available to him? According to Jones' biographer, Jefferson wanted to keep Jones active and gaining new battle experience until America could create its own fleet. I believe Jefferson was also intrigued in Jones' potential adversary. The Ottoman Empire controlled three of the four Barbary states: Algiers, Tripoli, and Tunis. Britain, a Protestant nation, controlled three key naval ports on the outskirts of Catholic Europe: Gibraltar, Minorca, and Malta. To balance its sea power, it used trade-offs with Turkey and the Barbary republics. So, why shouldn't America, in turn, quietly assist Russia in making life difficult for Turks?

In May 1788, Jones set out for Saint Petersburg, keeping Jefferson updated via correspondence. He saw Empress Catherine and gave her a copy of the recently ratified United States Constitution. His years in Russia were to be particularly difficult since he became entangled in the empress's court's ruthless intrigues, but he did see some significant service in the Black Sea and managed to inflict some heavy blows on the Turkish navy. He appears to have advocated an alliance between the United States and Russia against the Mediterranean pirates on his own initiative. He also advocated "going to the source" and commanding a Russian fleet into the Mediterranean to assault Ottoman trade between Constantinople and Egypt. The Dey of Algiers put a price on his head for these and other impertinences on the side of the unbelievers.

Jones eventually returned to Paris, where he died in lonely and squalid circumstances in July 1792, after being undermined in Russia by his rivals, falling out of favor with the empress, and suffering from jaundice and nephritis. By this time, Jefferson had been replaced as minister in Paris by Gouverneur Morris, who was as disappointed and irritated with Jones's effects as he had been with the imprisoned Thomas Paine. Just after Jones's death, a packet addressed to him came from the State Department. It included Jefferson's invitation. He wanted Jones to lead a delegation to Algiers, threatening the Dey with terrible consequences if his extortion strategy persisted, and he had convinced George Washington to sign a commission for Jones to do so.

Jefferson stepped down as Secretary of State in 1793. But the Barbary issue had taken on a life of its own by that point. The condition of American captives in North African jails, which had been the topic of several of Jones' letters to Jefferson, had become a major concern in the United States. Not only were they subjected to abhorrent treatment, but they were also threatened with forceful conversion to Islam and, it was rumored, sexual activities too repulsive to describe. Their pitiful letters from prison sparked widespread public outrage, prompting Congress to commission six frigates for the Barbary coast in 1794. Three of these were actually built: the United States, the Constitution, and the Constellation.

America was getting a permanent navy, even if, in a historical irony and contradiction, it was mostly Jeffersonian Republicans who opposed the cost of such a force, as well as the violation of the cherished prohibition on standing armies that it meant. However, as on previous occasions, Jefferson had been removed from the immediate political struggle and was in "retirement" at Monticello, where he was busy developing his collection. In 1790, he issued a telegram to Congress titled "Proposal to Use Force Against the Barbary States," in which he willed the end while leaving the methods to others. In his absence, his favorite cause gained credibility by association. It profited from increased federal income (particularly those earned by the despised whiskey tax), as well as Federalist enmity to France during the "quasi-war" with French privateers. As a result, when James Madison rose to speak in opposition to the massive new naval appropriations of 1794, the moral head of his Republican side, safe in Virginia, was able to maintain a sphinx-like silence. When the "XYZ" issue erupted four years later, sparking new calls for rearmament and against "tribute," Vice President Jefferson was able to reconcile fury against France with enduring suspicion of Britain's hidden hand in the Mediterranean, as he had done with the Genet catastrophe. By the time he took office, he was in command of not just a modern fleet, well-built by John Adams, but also the United States Marine Corps, founded in July 1798.

Jefferson's long-planned ruthlessness against the Barbary powers—he even considered kidnapping their sailors in reprisal and selling them at Malta's vast Christian-run slave market—was given ample time to manifest itself by the pashas' avarice and incompetence. The ruler of Tripoli, Yusuf Karamanli, had been foolish enough to deliver an ultimatum to the United States in late 1800, threatening war if his exorbitant terms were not met. President Jefferson, in fact, decided to take this latent declaration of war at face value. He obtained agreement from his cabinet on the dispatch of a squadron and resolved not to bother Congress with the matter. Its members were in recess anyway, but surely the president had the ability to act alone in times of war? The fleet was on the high seas only three months after Jefferson's inauguration, and Jefferson did not notify Congress until the warships had sailed far enough to be practically beyond recall.

The Barbary coast was effectively "pacified" during the next four years by a unilateral American mission, which the president laconically described as a continuous "cruise." Algeria, Morocco, and Tunis eventually withdrew their cooperation with the Pasha of Tripoli as a result of bombardment or the threat of it. Yusuf, on the other hand, remained obstinate, even daring to board and seize the USS Philadelphia in 1803.

Henry Adams was old enough, and had previously been young enough, to celebrate the names of the American heroes whose exploits had been the material of his youth reading when he came to write his brilliant study of the Jefferson administrations. Two particular instances, ending in the victory of American arms, are still remembered. Captain Stephen Decatur sailed right into Tripoli harbor in February 1804. Instead of allowing it to remain in Barbary hands, the captured Philadelphia was set on fire. Decatur returned in August, assaulting the defended town, boarding the pasha's own fleet where it lay at anchor, and liberating the crew of the Philadelphia from a horrific incarceration. According to folklore and several eyewitnesses, Decatur murdered the Muslim warrior who had previously killed his brother, Lieutenant James Decatur. In April of the following year, youthful Captain William Eaton led a combined army of Arabs, mercenaries, and American marines on a desert march from inland that took Derna, the second city of Tripoli (today's Libya). Lieutenant Presley O'Bannon raised the American flag over the defeated town, marking the first time the flag had been planted in battle on a foreign shore. This occasion is retained in the Marine anthem's opening line, "From the halls of Montezuma to the shores of Tripoli."

Because they occurred so soon after the Louisiana Purchase, these triumphs and their great monetary cost (together with the war's "presidential" and somewhat covert nature) drew significant Federalist criticism. However, there was no arguing with success. It took a bit longer for all of the Barbary states to sign treaties with the US, pledging to stop piracy and kidnapping. In Washington, the Tunisian envoy, Sidi Soliman Melli Melli, intended to be entertained at the expense of the public with the companionship of several women of the night. (To demonstrate their familiarity with the reality of life, Jefferson and Madison set up an off-the-record State Department fund for this specific reason.) More punitive expeditions against Algiers were needed in the coming years, but Jefferson's policy was essentially a triumph for peace and the independence of trade from extortion through the use of deliberate force. The United States' prestige was greatly boosted, and Decatur's battle-tested navy was to distinguish itself in even more harsh warfare during the War of 1812.

Having had no real role in Haitian affairs since resigning as secretary of state in 1793, Jefferson's animosity and fear of the slave uprising had not abated. Without Jefferson's approval or cooperation, the Adams administration had been generally supportive of Haitian independence from France. This represented both the antislavery stance of prominent Federalist New Englanders, such as Secretary of State Timothy Pickering, and their deep antipathy for the French. Jefferson's presidency was markedly different. He supported French efforts to retake control of Haiti, with the implication that this would lead to the return of slavery, not only because he detested slave revolts, but also because he thought that this would expand American trade with the island and the rest of the Caribbean basin.

One could argue that Jefferson was betraying even his professed principles on slavery and colorism. He recommended emancipating American slaves and transporting them to Africa or the West Indies. This concept, known colloquially as "colonization," was predicated on there being some nearby black-ruled territory where slaves could go or be sent. However, when it came down to it, Jefferson denied Haitians the right to establish such a state. One of Jefferson's harshest opponents, historian Michael Zuckerman, used the Exodus metaphor to sum up Jefferson's attitude toward slaves: "Even as he yearned to get rid of them, he refused to let them go."

However, Napoleon's suppression of the French Revolution enabled Jefferson to be far more pragmatic in dealing with France and England. In his first meeting with French ambassador Louis Pichon in July 1801, he even urged that the two warring powers make peace and restore order in the Caribbean together. He undoubtedly gave Napoleon and his foreign minister Talleyrand the notion that

American assistance would be accessible to France in any case. This assurance was crucial to the French, and it had recently grown in importance. Something unusual had occurred in Haiti. Toussaint L'Ouverture had emerged as a superb rebel general, arguably the first slave leader since the possibly mythical Spartacus. Toussaint had declared the first black-ruled republic in history, massing slaves behind him in a powerful army. Napoleon, who had no desire for peace with England, anticipated that a decisive action would reestablish French authority in the transatlantic region and so earn new funds for his even grander imperial scheme. In October 1801 he sent an army and a navy to Haiti under the command of General Leclerc.

C. L. R. James' masterwork The Black Jacobins tells the narrative of that expedition's loss and almost annihilation at the hands of a slave phalanx. The French army and navy were effectively destroyed by the principles of the French revolution (although with some assistance from sickness). Toussaint was eventually apprehended, transferred to France, imprisoned in a cold cell in the French Pyrenees, and allowed to die of neglect. In the meantime, Napoleon's hopes for re-establishing French dominance in the region had been dashed. And his shattered army and ships in Haiti never gained the American assistance and sympathy they had hoped for.

Jefferson imagined a future America that stretched from Florida to at least Cuba, and then west of the Mississippi as far as it could go. This outcome was dependent on two factors: the deft managing of rivalry between England, France, and Spain, and the birth of a sufficient number of people to supply settlers in the new regions.

As in the case of the Barbary states, Jefferson clearly believed that the American imperative had been pondered and rehearsed for long enough, and that the time for pitiless decision had come. It is unclear whether the French believed his threat of an alliance with Britain, but it is safe to say that both Napoleon and Talleyrand, for possibly different reasons, needed immediate gold in order to continue their wars against Great Britain and Russia. Even before Monroe could take his seat at the bargaining table to haggle over the original offer of ten million dollars for New Orleans, the French side returned to

Livingston with a new offer. Fifteen million dollars would purchase all of the American territory that France had to sell: an area so vast that its true size was unknown. (When Livingston asked Talleyrand how much area was involved, he was met with a shrug and the response, "I can't give you any direction." You've struck a fine bargain for yourself, and I'm sure you'll make the most of it." What a fitting retaliation for the XYZ team's attempted extortion.) At the time, the best estimate was that the United States had about doubled its area of sovereignty at a cost of four cents per acre.

In truth, it was far from apparent that such a significant private agreement was the "logical outcome" of the Constitution's adoption. Jefferson handled this vexing subject with his trademark pedantry and suppleness. He first carefully reviewed the Constitution, but was unable to find any provision that would allow the federal government to purchase new national territory or spend the necessary funds without consent. (He must have remembered, perhaps with displeasure or embarrassment, his strong remark that Alexander Hamilton could not even establish a national bank under the Constitution.)

However, two rumors pressed Jefferson's hand and drove his quick abandoning of constitutional niceties. Napoleon was thought to be contemplating the appropriateness of his bargain, and it was also understood that the Spanish authorities might oppose the proposed deal's premise, claiming that no one had specified the proper limits of Louisiana. Jefferson had already determined that the Spanish-owned Florida territories could be added to the acquisition in due course, and that even if Madrid would not sell now, "as soon as she is at war, we push them strongly with one hand, holding out a price with the other, we shall certainly obtain the Floridas." General Andrew Jackson would subsequently validate this forecast; in the meantime, it was necessary to get the signatures of France and the United States Senate on what had been gained in Paris. Thus, almost without pausing for air, Jefferson shifted to the position that "the less that is said about my constitutional difficulty, the better; and that it will be desirable for Congress to do what is necessary in silence."

He anticipated that a bold act of national aggrandizement like this would elicit enormous public support. He also predicted that it would put the Federalists on the defensive. On both counts, he was correct. The sheer scope and audacity of the venture gained widespread approval, and the Senate awarded him an overwhelming majority after a brief debate. When the pact was signed, Robert Livingston most likely spoke for the majority when he said, "From this day, the United States take their place among the powers of first rank." (Note the locution: it wasn't until after Gettysburg that Americans started saying "the United States is" rather than "the United States are.") Meanwhile, Alexander Hamilton remarked sarcastically that the Purchase should be attributed to "the kind interpositions of an overruling Providence," while much of the New England Federalist press suddenly became strictly and literally constructionist, mocking the bargain as an exchange of precious cold cash, of which the United States already had too little, for land, of which it already had too much. On the subject of the constitution, John Quincy Adams was even more emphatic. He claimed that the president would now be dealing with "an assumption of implied power greater...than all of the assumptions of implied power in the years of the Washington and Adams administrations combined." This criticism had the merit of being true, as Jefferson happily recognized.

He recommended that the new province be governed, at least initially, by an appointed governor and an unelected "Assembly of Notables." In his letters, he spoke to his new subjects in the same manner that imperial proconsuls had always done: he portrayed them as "children" who needed to be nurtured to adulthood. (In a move that may have reflected his terrible conscience on this matter, he asked the Marquis de Lafayette, a French reformer with democratic aspirations, to take over as governor of Louisiana.)

The administrative and constitutional concerns paled in comparison to the crucial issue that plagued Jefferson throughout his career. He had to answer the question: Would the great sin of slavery be extinguished further by this massive acquisition, or would it at least be attenuated? He had secured New Orleans and the Mississippi by the rather unsentimental expedient of betraying the revolution in Haiti as well as double-crossing France.

This is not one of those concerns about slavery that are only raised in retrospect or by a more easily shocked generation. It was obvious and widely debated at the time. Thomas Paine, who had pushed Jefferson to make the Louisiana Purchase without realizing it, pleaded with him to keep slavery out of the new territory and to establish German migrants instead of black slaves. James Hillhouse of Connecticut, a Federalist congressman, submitted an amendment to the Louisiana law to safeguard the territory from the practice, which was enthusiastically backed by Joel Barlow, who, like Paine, was a personal friend of Jefferson. In theory, morality, and law, the case was no different from Jefferson's proposed restriction of any extension of slavery in the Northwest ordinance of 1787. However, the sugar industry succeeded in 1804, just as the cotton industry did later. Louisiana, as Paine claimed, would produce more sugar in the long run if populated by hardworking Germans, but it would produce less sugar in the short run if slavery were abolished, and competitor producers in the West Indies would exploit the advantage. So the president would only agree to a prohibition on the purchase of imported slaves, a step toward the elimination of the foreign slave trade in January 1808.

Jefferson's crucial and deliberate refusal to broaden the vision of abolition resulted in the admission of Louisiana as a slave state, followed by the admission of states formed from the larger territory of the Purchase, so that by 1819 there were twenty-two states in the Union, eleven with slavery and eleven without: precisely the contradiction of "half slave and half free" that would later trouble Mr. Lincoln. Missouri, the next state founded from Louisiana territory, was to tip the scales.

Since Jefferson could scarcely have been ignorant that his Louisiana diplomacy had seriously jeopardized three of his most valued principles—slavery abolition, the renowned Republican style of democracy, and the Union's integrity—it is reasonable to wonder what motivated him to take the risk. The solution is straightforward. He was aware of something that neither his Federalist adversaries nor his Republican allies were. He had been contemplating and planning an adventure to the West for several years. And it must have given him great delight on the day he dispatched Lewis and Clark in July 1803 to be able to tell them that the Indian leaders they would meet now owed their allegiance to a new country. To an extent that could not have been predicted, the "uncharted" regions were already a part of the United States.

Again, the seed of the idea was present during Jefferson's diplomatic visit to Paris, if not slightly earlier. In 1783, he invited General George Rodgers Clark, a frontier hero, to travel as a scout into the West, but the general declined. Two years later, while serving in Paris, Jefferson discovered that King Louis was preparing an expedition to the Pacific Northwest led by Comte La Perouse. Despite official French assurances that the expedition was solely scientific in nature, Jefferson and John Paul Jones decided that Paris was interested in creating colonies on the continent's western edge. The following year, Jefferson met a strange adventurer named John Ledyard, who had sailed with Captain James Cook and was the first American to visit the Pacific Northwest. Ledyard devised a wild plan to journey across European Russia, cross Siberia, bridge the Bering Strait, and walk across the continent to the East Coast to deliver his report. Jefferson supported him in this endeavor, which did not bear fruit in the same manner that Jones' posting to Russia had. (Empress Catherine apprehended and deported Ledyard as soon as he arrived in Siberia.)

But because the expedition commanded by Comte La Perouse never returned—its wreckage was discovered decades later on a Pacific island—the subject of the interior and the West remained unresolved when Jefferson became Secretary of State. In 1792, he accepted the French scientist André Michaux's invitation to investigate the origins and outlets of the American river system. Michaux, on the other hand, proved to be part naturalist and half agent, bringing the research to a premature end due to his connections with French interests and French espionage.

The connection with French initiative (and the necessity to anticipate it) is intriguing. Napoleon Bonaparte used the help of historians, cartographers, botanists, linguists, anthropologists, and builders to smooth his way and expand his power during his legendary occupation of Egypt at the end of the nineteenth century. Most scholars trace European Orientalism back to this grandiose, intellectual, yet imperial intent. Jefferson was aware that the Americans would not be confronted with massive armies or old towns as they traveled westward, but he was also concerned with making the trip a mission of learning as well as charting and acquisition. He also desired an internal market to offset reliance on the Atlantic Ocean and the unpredictable powers that still governed it. His scheme could be described as "Occidentalist."

In the back of his mind was also the unavoidable question of the tobacco-and-slavery economy, on which his own standing depended and which he knew was doomed. The colonial economy was rich in land but poor in cash—Hamilton was technically correct on this point—and it was also labor-intensive while lacking in capital. The "small tobacco" technique was wasteful and promiscuous in terms of agriculture, draining goodness from the soil in quest of a short-term yield. Longer-term management, such as crop rotation and soil care, would have resulted in less short-term profitability. In his Notes on the State of Virginia, Jefferson half-confronted this dilemma, arguing in a rare concession to European superiority that American agricultural inadequacy arose "from our having such quantities of land to waste as we please." In Europe, the goal is to make the most of their land because labor is plentiful; here, the goal is to make the most of our labor because land is plentiful."

Jefferson, like many others who split the moral divide on slavery as it played out in everyday politics, justified himself by believing that a younger generation would cleanse the inherited stain, and that the expansion of America would "diffuse" the slave system until it shrank and died of its own accord. This mix of idealism and cynicism runs throughout the Lewis and Clark tale. When Jefferson met and trained young Virginians and Kentuckians like Meriwether Lewis or William Clark (the younger brother of General George Rodgers Clark), he made no attempt to persuade them of the merits of emancipation, according to Stephen Ambrose.

In any event, the work of discovery took primacy. Because no one knew how far northward the alleged Missouri line actually ran, the terms of the Louisiana Purchase had to be vague. This effectively allowed Jefferson free rein. But, as with the Purchase, he did not feel comfortable disclosing his intentions to Congress in advance. Funding would be required, although it is unlikely that it would be forthcoming if another "botanizing expedition" was planned. The heroic lie that the president planned to tell the legislative branch was based on an advantage he gained by losing his last struggle with Hamilton: the Constitution does, in fact, provide for the funding of an expedition devoted to the expansion of commerce. Given the extensive fur trade in the interior, it was not difficult for the president to gain the attention of a significant number of congressmen. Perhaps anticipating this, he mixed some truth with his deception and declared, "The interests of commerce place the principal object within the constitutional powers and cares of Congress, and that it should incidentally advance geographical knowledge of our own continent cannot but be an additional gratification." With this bribery, he extracted a grand total of $2,500 from Congress for the most historic exploration in contemporary history.

In 1940, the first full year of his exile in the United States, W. H. Auden produced a long and exquisite poem titled "New Year Letter." In it, he likened America's vastness and freedom to the sadness and staleness of Old Europe.

The lyrics in German that say "no ruined castles, no marble columns" are borrowed from Goethe's poem "Amerika, du hast es besser" (America, you have it better).
Auden had also definitely been reading Henry Adams, who wrote extensively in his articles on Europe and America about the tension between the Virgin and the dynamo.

The prevalent perception of America as a new Eden or virgin continent, with a new creation of plants and animals waiting to be discovered, was tempered to some extent by the realization that the human species had already arrived. For many of the advancing or encroaching white settlers, this was merely a nuisance. And for many aboriginal peoples, who had no way of knowing what a dynamo engine of productivity and creativity was beginning to spin on an eastern shore they had never seen before, the presence of European interlopers was just another tribal rivalry to be settled through conventional means.

Despite the harsh terms he had used in framing the Declaration, Jefferson grew anxious to appease the Indians. And it's worth noting that, at least in this situation, he exhibited none of the bigotry or race theory that was so prevalent at the time. The racism was that of despised and sometimes fearful white settlers, and the racial theory was that of Buffon and his colleagues, who considered native Americans were useless. In contrast, Jefferson believed that red skin was the natural equal of white skin in every way. All they had to do was learn to farm, free their women from labor, intermarry with Europeans, and reject the harmful ideas of their priests, shamans, and witch doctors.

He created a special room at Monticello for the gathering and study of Indian cultural items, and he was particularly interested in Indian languages and vocabularies, of which he amassed an enormous collection that is now lost to us. He advocated that the legal penalty for killing an Indian be the same as the penalty for killing a white man. The delight he got in being referred to as the Great White Chief, or Father, and in entertaining delegations of lesser chiefs at the White House was the closest he ever came to indulgent monarchical fantasies. In fact, his outfitting of the Lewis and Clark expedition was a reversal of traditional philosophy of royal training. Alexander of Macedon was tutored by Aristotle, whereas the Florentine monarchs were tutored by Machiavelli. However, Lewis and Clark were educated by a president. It's even possible that Jefferson taught Meriwether Lewis to read and write, or at least to an acceptable level.

Few nuances were neglected in this education. Lewis was dispatched to Philadelphia, the home of Jefferson's favorite American Philosophical Society, to meet such distinguished scientists and physicians as Dr. Benjamin Rush. From Benjamin Barton and Caspar Wistar, he learned the fundamentals of astronomy and navigation, as well as the natural sciences. He was taught the Jenner method of smallpox vaccination, in which Jefferson was a firm believer, and urged to disseminate the concept among the tribes he visited. So it's not too much of a stretch to say that the Lewis and Clark expedition was designed as an Enlightenment endeavor, aimed as much at spreading knowledge as it was at acquiring knowledge, and of the power that knowledge would, of course, bring.

The inexact state of knowledge at the time, as well as the hypotheses that arose, prompted much political criticism from the Federalist side. Jefferson was portrayed as a lunatic who believed in mythical creatures and the presence of giants and monsters. (In truth, he did not completely dismiss some interior reports.) However, as word of the vastness and diversity of the true West spread, the Federalists were made to appear little, or, perhaps more accurately, to appear as if they had been thinking small—as they had in the case of Louisiana.

The dignity of the expansionist and exploratory effort was preserved for a time. Several of the Indian tribes received Lewis and Clark with friendliness and assistance, mixed with suspicion and opposition. And some of the tribes or nations accepted Jefferson's invitation to coexist. He appears to have had a special fondness for people whose names began with the letter C: Cherokees, Choctaws, Chickasaws, and Creeks, the latter of whom actually petitioned for citizenship, while the Cherokees began to settle down, develop a written language, and publish a newspaper. This lofty and "improving" era, which was not without condescension and paternalism on the white side, is now forced to be regarded through the reverse lens of later horrors and butcheries. The concept of assimilation quickly gave way to its always implied and no less Jeffersonian alternative—"Indian removal," to use a crude euphemism of the period. Some argue that Meriwether Lewis's suicide in 1809, caused by a lethal combination of alcohol, snuff, and manic despair, was the last point at which the transition from Jeffersonian to Jacksonian could have been avoided. (In other words, Lewis's celebrity may have aided in the arrest.)

As a result, Thomas Jefferson doubled the size of the United States and laid the groundwork for its future completion as a bicoastal and continental power. (His discussions with Ledyard in Paris concerning the Bering Strait foreshadowed Seward's later conquest of Alaska.) In the medium term, however, his tactics sustained and maintained the "unusual institution" of slavery, subjected native Americans to quick and cruel encroachment, and, with his ambitions in the Caribbean and beyond, promoted the enticing ideals of "manifest destiny" and colonial expansion.

Chapter 8:
Disappointment: The Second Term

In some ways, Jefferson's first administration's triumph was a celebration of his past setbacks. He used Hamilton's financial system, Adams' military and naval strength, the once-disliked Atlantic alliance with Britain, and even the premise of the Alien and Sedition Acts in one trial of a Federalist journalist in New York named Harry Crosswell. Some would call this opportunism, and not without reason. His supporters may argue that he learned from his blunders. He obviously knew how to profit from other people's mistakes, and he was quite capable of retaining a fixed thought and patiently waiting for the time of vindication.

At the unfortunate conference in 1786 between King George III, Jefferson, and Adams, the Hanoverian king could not have predicted that an upstart ex-colonist from Virginia would become the president of a powerful country. He might have been more polite if he could have imagined such a possibility. In any case, his rudeness on that occasion—"the ulcerations in the narrow mind of that mulish being," in Jefferson's words—would irritate him for years to come.

Anthony Merry, the British envoy to Washington, was the target of the delayed retort. After a break in relations between the two countries, he arrived in November 1803 to deliver his credentials. The exquisite social torments prepared for him, and the damage done to Anglo-American ties as a result, would require the more novelistic pen of a Henry Adams. The Merrys (including the ambassador's lady) had a tough time finding adequate accommodations or servants in a metropolis that was dreary and provincial even by less pretentious standards. When Merry went to see Jefferson, accompanied by James Madison, he found the formal reception area empty at first.

This was really a dress rehearsal for Thomas Jefferson's dinner party a few nights later. The Merrys arrived at the White House believing that the event was being thrown in their honor. They may have disregarded the obnoxious presence of the French chargé Louis Pichon, an emissary from an opposing state. They may have forgiven

Jefferson for allowing his guests to take their seats at dinner at random, without regard for precedent or seniority. These were common occurrences during presidential soirees. But when Jefferson gave Dolley Madison his arm—over her protests—and led her into supper, leaving Mrs. Merry to make whatever adjustment she could, they had little choice but to make the worst of things. Any remaining concerns were removed when Napoleon's younger brother, Jerome Bonaparte, visited Washington a short time later to show off his gorgeous American bride, Elizabeth Patterson. When dinner was served, Jefferson graciously extended his arm to this lady.

On New Year's Day 1804, an already irritated Merry paid another courtesy visit to the White House, only to find Jefferson engrossed in conversation with three visiting Indian chieftains. He barely interrupted this exchange to acknowledge his British visitor, at which point Merry stormed off, protesting that "painted savages" were being preferred to a representative of His Britannic Majesty. He would have been even more enraged if he had discovered Jefferson's disdain for his wife in a letter to James Monroe, the American diplomat in London at the time. (She had, he observed, "established a degree of dislike among all classes which one would have thought impossible in so short a time."

There were historical ramifications to the outcome of this grudge bout when, later in 1804, Merry had the opportunity for vengeance and took it with zeal. In a fascinating incident that historians still debate, he was approached by none other than Jefferson's vice president, Aaron Burr. Despite the opprobrium—and the legal indictments from two states—that had fallen on him after his duel with Alexander Hamilton that July, this inveterate old rake and opportunist had remained to preside coolly over the Senate. ("I never indeed thought of him as an honest, frank-dealing man," Jefferson later said of his two-time—and two-timing—running buddy, "but considered him as a crooked gun or other perverted machine, whose aim you could never be sure of." The poor metaphor of Burr's precision as a marksman appears doubly terrible; nonetheless, he has been politically valuable since the "botanizing excursion." His official prospects and usefulness were now over: his party pulled him from the ticket for Jefferson's reelection campaign in 1804 (which he handily won with Governor George Clinton as running mate).

Burr had decided to reinvent himself as the leader of a secessionist insurrection in the western states, anticipating his impending obsolescence in electoral politics. If successful, Burr pointed out to Merry, this scheme could blend with other freebooters' fantasies of conquering the Floridas and even Mexico. In any case, it would be a devastating blow to the increasingly ascendant Jefferson and the enormous but insecure new American dominions of the Louisiana Purchase. Merry eagerly conveyed the concept to London because British money and vessels would be required. At a later meeting in late 1805, after Burr had returned from a reconnaissance expedition, he informed Merry that preparations for an insurrection were underway, and that if Britain did not take advantage of them, France would fill the void. Merry appears to have failed to pique London's attention in this idea. His superiors were more concerned with the European theater of Napoleon's war. Burr then turned to Spain, which was still bitter at the loss of the colonies.

The remarkable twists and turns of the Burr affair continue to fascinate historians (and authors like Gore Vidal, whose fictionalized depiction of the incident includes a striking portrayal of Jefferson). It's unclear how ambitious Burr was, how closely entangled he was with Spain, or how much he encouraged mutiny from General James Wilkinson, who commanded American forces in the Southwest. The certainty is that his quixotry (or banditry) had some attraction for frontier settlers who despised or distrusted the federal government and respected the guy who had murdered Alexander Hamilton, the banker's friend. Jefferson had expressed little or no grief over Hamilton's murder, but Burr's was a direct threat to his power that he could not afford to ignore. Apart from anything else, Lewis and Clark were still on their mission, as he knew and most others did not. The fate of the alarmingly loose, frantically expanding new union was in doubt. In November 1806, President Thomas Jefferson issued an arrest warrant for Aaron Burr on treasonous accusations.

There was a brief interlude of alternating drama and farce, with a scramble on the Burr-Wilkinson wing to switch sides while there was still time. Rather than wait for this to take effect, Jefferson told Congress that Burr's guilt was "placed beyond question." This observation should have been made after the trial rather than before it, especially since jurisdictional issues made it unclear if a proper trial could be held at all. An indictment for treason and conspiracy was presented in March 1807 at the Fourth Circuit Court in Richmond, Virginia, following a comedy of errors involving Burr's detention, release, and re-arrest in Mississippi—events the proto-defendant milked to the maximum with his characteristic grace.

Any joy Jefferson felt at witnessing the arraignment of this cunning monster vanished quickly. The case was assigned to Chief Justice John Marshall, who had so thoroughly embarrassed the Republicans in the "XYZ" business and whose political preferences were widely publicized. Soon after the trial began, Marshall dismissed the major accusation of treason, which was difficult to prove in any case because it required direct testimony concerning overt activities. This left the court to consider whether Burr had conspired to invade a friendly power's territory: Mexico. Burr, emboldened, demanded a subpoena compelling the president to testify as a witness and produce all papers pertinent to his case. This request was granted by Justice Marshall, much to Jefferson's chagrin, and he became the first chief executive to invoke executive privilege and other immunities. As a result, the defense withdrew the demand for Jefferson's own appearance, and they were rewarded with enough government paperwork to make their job easier. In the face of legal and political ambiguity, the jury reached the same conclusion, declaring Burr "not proved to be guilty under this indictment by any evidence submitted to us." With its resonance of the Scottish alternative of "not proven," this did not quite clear Burr's name. But clean bills were probably less important to him than his liberty, and he went to Europe for the next five years before returning to New York and continuing his legal career, as well as many of his old immoral habits.

When the British Royal Navy committed a flagrant act of aggression in June 1807, while Jefferson was being subpoenaed by Burr's defense team, a lesser man could have been tempted to demagogy. The USS Chesapeake, on its way to the Mediterranean, was stopped by HMS Leopard off the coast of Virginia's Hampton Roads and ordered to submit to a search. When this command was refused, the Chesapeake was raked with multiple fatal broadsides, boarded, and four crew men were relieved. The pretext, as much as the conduct itself, sparked a firestorm of indignation in American society. The United Kingdom reserved the authority to disrupt American marine activity, whether navy or civilian, in order to "impress" new crew members or to recover those who had escaped British service. Jefferson had despatched James Monroe and William Pinckney to London the previous year to renegotiate the 1795 John Jay pact as it related to the subject of "impressment." The experiment had failed. As bad as this was, just one of the four men apprehended on the Chesapeake had been a "deserter" at all. The other three were American citizens who had fled from the army. The deserter was hung at Halifax, Canada, while the other three were pardoned on the condition that they reenlist under the British banner.

The outpouring of rage throughout the country as a whole, and its unanimity among both Republicans and Federalists, combined long-standing and well-understood concerns with new and provocative ones, meant that Jefferson might easily have achieved a declaration of war. He chose to play a lengthier game, however. Envoys were sent to London to demand reparation, while news from Europe was kept quiet. Jefferson, having lost most of his romantic notions about France, was unwilling to go in war on either side of the Anglo-French conflict. He was more interested in profiting from the outcome of that argument. This created a mental difficulty for him. On the one hand, "I suppose our fate will be determined by Bonaparte's successes or failures." It is quite repugnant that we should be forced to wish Bonaparte victory and seek to his victims for salvation." However, as he put it, the British were "as tyrannical at sea as [Bonaparte] is on land." He resolved this disagreement by preparing for battle while negotiating for peace. A militia was gathered in preparation for an invasion on Canada (the familiar dream reappeared). And the thirst for the South surfaced once more, since war would provide another opportunity to end the Spanish presence once and for all. "Our southern defensive force can take the Floridas, and volunteers for a Mexican army will flock to our banner... Probably Cuba will join our confederation." In other words, the great cause of American growth would not be left to greedy individual amateurs like Aaron Burr if it came to that.

Meanwhile, George Canning, the Tory foreign secretary, scorned Jefferson's "two-track" approach, which prohibited the British navy from using American seas while pursuing the return of the kidnapped seamen and resolving the long-standing impressment issue. He saw Britain as the aggrieved party in the situation, and defended the Crown's "Orders in Council" under which the Crown claimed the right to prohibit any commerce at any moment in pursuance of its blockade of Bonaparte. Jefferson then made two decisions that would define his final years in office. First, in December 1807, he declared that he would not run for president again: a significant act of renunciation in the circumstances. Second, later that month, he requested that Congress approve the Embargo Act. Both houses gave him solid majorities. For the first time in modern history, the energy and unity that would have backed a war policy were diverted into a campaign of peaceful sanctions. No American vessels could now sail to foreign ports, and no foreign vessels could load in American ports. This technique was foreshadowed in Jefferson's report on non-belligerent methods available to the United States as secretary of state following the Genet debacle.

Unfortunately for humanity, the sacrifice that a nation will make for a lengthy conflict is sometimes greater than the sacrifice that it will make for a protracted peace. Jefferson's doctrine, which attempted to bring both belligerent countries to their senses (and French raiders had long preyed on American shipping), was quickly discredited. The high-mindedness was harmed by the harsh necessity of execution and enforcement, and the impartiality was tainted by the notion that the embargo was aimed more at Britain than at France. Both objections were reasonable. At the Treasury, Albert Gallatin was pushed to close more and more loopholes in the embargo system. New restrictions and officials had to prohibit smuggling along the Canadian border, which was a hugely popular local hobby. Ship captains and port authorities had to be reminded that there were no exceptions for unloading or loading particular profitable goods. Many Americans' libertarian spirits were harmed, as were their wallets, and the historic image of the repressive British exciseman was still fresh enough to be freely invoked. Perhaps paradoxically, it was also claimed that the embargo was anti-French and was the result of a secret collaboration between Jefferson and Bonaparte. Unemployed seafarers banded together with New England Federalists in an uprising accusing Jefferson of taking bread from the mouths of laboring Americans. (The metaphor of "bread" was simple to use because Jefferson had put himself in the role of a socialist rationcard bureaucrat by deciding to arbitrate the permissible types of flour.)

Jefferson's private goal was that, in addition to giving Old Europe a lesson, the embargo would boost import substitution, encourage industry and business in the interior of the country, and teach Americans to rely less on foreigners. Indeed, local industry received a significant boost, particularly in Pennsylvania. In the short term, farmers began to stockpile, sailors and merchants rebelled, and attorneys and customs authorities litigated ceaselessly or accepted bribes. On top of that, Jefferson's plan to use regular army and navy men to guard land and maritime routes was easily viewed as a panic measure: authoritarianism replacing idealism.

There was also some substance to the charge that the embargo was biased. Jefferson recognized that the British were more susceptible since they were an island nation with more ships and colonies. He believed that greater effort would have resulted in British capitulation until the end of his days. And it is undeniably true that the embargo measures, while attesting to America's greater economic power, caused significant hardship and disruption in British markets. Meanwhile, Napoleon Bonaparte more than lived up to Jefferson's negative assessment of him. He chose to view the embargo as effectively pro-British, issuing decrees that regarded all American ships in European ports as if they were traveling under British flag. The only diplomatic consolation was an improvement in relations between the US and Napoleon's adversary Russia, which exchanged ambassadors shortly after.

In November 1808, Jefferson's preferred candidate, James Madison, won the presidential election with a significant, albeit diminished, Republican majority in the Electoral College. This may be interpreted as a conditional support for the embargo. However, the enterprise's mainspring appeared to have broken, and when Congress had a chance to vote the following March, it replaced the Embargo Act with the considerably weakened Non-Intercourse Act. There would be no further American pacifist-internationalist involvement in European politics until Woodrow Wilson's presidency almost a century later.

And the path to the War of 1812 was clear.

Jefferson's self-pity could not be accused of masking any future ambition this time. And his use of the high seas image, as prevalent as it was, may be excused in this context.

Without fully comprehending it, or perhaps intending it, Jefferson had aided in the passage of the United States from colonial settlement to continental nationhood. He had also given it (or them) influence in international councils. This had come at a cost to his idealized ideals of agrarianism and communitarianism, as well as a significant cost to the delicate relationship between the federal Constitution and the states. Unresolved issues included involuntary servitude, the precise limits of the new nation, and the fate of non-European tribes. However, these issues needed to be addressed in the context of an increasingly aggressive American modernism.

Chapter 9:
Declining Years

Jefferson's final return to Virginia did not represent the transformation of the United States into a modern or outward-looking civilization that he had oversaw. He never left the state again, limiting himself mostly to agriculture and the production of handcrafted artifacts for the ornamentation and improvement of his house and land. He did, however, continue to play a role in the life of his country. Education and secularism were two topics that dominated his final years, and they proved to be inextricably linked, often in unsettling ways. And there was always, always, always the taint and shadow of slavery.

Jefferson considered the foundation of the University of Virginia to be one of just three of his accomplishments worthy of remembrance on his own tombstone. The university also represented the culmination of his evangelistic interest in general education that he had demonstrated as a young Virginia politician. I purposely chose the word proselytize because it was his clear desire to establish a campus free of all priests and denominations. Perhaps for this reason, he requested that it be built partly under his supervision, in the little town of Charlottesville, which bordered Monticello, and that its architectural plan be classical, rather than the quasi-Gothic form of so many Anglican or Episcopal universities. Palladian would be the style. There would be no divinity or theology chairs. Christianity would be studied alongside evolution and ethics. Students would be permitted to choose their own unique subjects rather than adhering to a prescribed curriculum. The building's design—an imposing Pantheon contrasted with an open lawn and a collection of structures that allowed students and instructors to be close together—was a combination of majesty and closeness. It was intended to be the Virginia branch of the global enlightenment, rather than a Virginian university. Only one chair, in law and government, was set aside for an American academic. To this day, most of the project's spacious yet elaborate architecture, with its porticos and columns, can be viewed with pleasure and instruction. However, the effort to build the site paled in comparison to the struggle to have it tenured, which began in 1819.

In the twenty-first century, the phrases scholarly and bureaucratic are nearly synonymous, and it comes as no surprise that Jefferson had to squander interminable time in committees and parochial fighting. Would his idea undermine the local clout of William and Mary College, his old mater? Would there be enough money? Would the location become a hotbed of rebellion and delinquency? The final question struck some of the petty-minded with a unique and powerful intensity. Thomas Cooper, Jefferson's chemistry nominee, would have been a credit to any university, anywhere, at any time. He worked closely with Dr. Joseph Priestley, the discoverer of oxygen. Priestley, an Englishman, had suffered greatly for his rationalism, faith in scientific method, and support for the American and French revolutions. His Birmingham laboratory had been shattered by an angry mob fueled by "Church and King" frenzy, that kind of mob rule sanctioned by the British crown and bishops as a weapon against Dissenters. (In one of his many errors, Edmund Burke approved of this hysteria, which was also directed towards Thomas Paine.) Not only had Priestley dabbled in profane experiments, but he had also established Unitarianism, which viewed Jesus of Nazareth as a mere mortal with ethical beliefs rather than the son of God. Dr. Cooper held the same opinion and had previously served time in prison under the Sedition Act. His scientific brilliance paled in comparison to the threat he posed to civility. At least, that's what the Virginian Presbyterians claimed. Their leader, John Holt Rice, added the extra and customary Pharisaic viewpoint that the appointment of an infidel would be rejected by the public. This was similar to the hypocritical argument Jefferson had faced four decades earlier during the debate for the Virginia Statute on Religious Freedom. On this time, he reacted even more forcefully to the Presbyterians. At one point, he claimed that all sects "dread the advance of science as witches do the approach of daylight; and scowl on the fatal harbinger announcing the subversion of the duperies in which they live." The Presbyterians, on the other hand, were "the most intolerant of all sects, the most tyrannical, and ambitious: ready, at the word of the lawgiver, if such a word could be obtained, to put the torch to the pile, and to rekindle in this virgin hemisphere the flames in which their oracle Calvin consumed the poor Servetus."

Merrill Peterson points out, with his usual sharpness and perspicuity, that Jefferson's fury, however brilliantly stated, showed a latent contradiction. There was supposed to be no conflict between democracy and the Enlightenment. The two were intended to march together, as they did against monarchy. Either you trusted "the people" or you didn't, and John Holt Rice had invoked majority sovereignty. In any case, Jefferson consented to rescind Dr. Cooper's appointment. Given Jefferson's advanced age in 1819, this could be considered a tactical retreat. And so may his tired awareness that attracting great intellectual talent from Europe, as he had long hoped, was too soon. However, in order to gain local and political support for the beloved university, he was willing to go one step farther and promote the Charlottesville lawn as a place where future defenders of slavery and states' rights may walk and converse.

The so-called Missouri Compromise of 1820 agreed to admit the Missouri territory (born of the Louisiana Purchase) as a slave state. This acquisition was "balanced" by the admittance of Maine, once a colony of Massachusetts, as a free state. This awkward deal sparked a massive uprising against slavery and its spread in the North. Much of the campaign was organized by former Tories and Federalists like Rufus King, whom Jefferson identified as historical and personal foes. He was not beyond making appeals to the Virginia legislature, arguing that Virginia needed its own institution to prevent northern colleges like Harvard from enticing its brightest sons. He claimed that up to 500 of the South's future leaders were being taught "anti-Missourism" and worse in the Northeast. "This canker is eating away at the very foundations of our existence, and if not stopped immediately, it will be irreversible." The "canker" to which he refers was the Unionist opposition to slavery. The concept of a "national university" had been quietly abandoned in favor of a sectional university. When it came down to it, Jefferson was for "Virginia First."

However, these and other techniques had the desired effect, and the institution was chartered and inaugurated by 1825. When the notion was still in its early stages, Jefferson boldly said, "This institution will be based on the illimitable freedom of the human mind." For here, we are not frightened to follow truth wherever it may lead, nor are we scared to tolerate error as long as reason is free to confront it." This echo of his first inauguration address indicated a bravery that was not matched by the outcome. Jefferson worked nervously to ensure that the obligatory political and constitutional documents were as traditional and Republican as possible.

Perhaps Jefferson was too successful in recruiting young swells eager to protect the old South; in any case, the campus's inauguration was quickly followed by the most raucous and sad type of student violence. Every kind of spoilt and selfish behavior was on display: eventually, the old guy had to ride painfully down the mountain to Charlottesville, and it is believed that his tears embarrassed the delinquents.

Regardless of how much his views, even on education, were influenced and colored by his protective attitude toward slavery, Jefferson's anticlericalism was most visible in the sphere of education. The War of 1812 was a disaster for the United States, far worse than Jefferson or anybody else could have predicted. In the early days of the conflict, he predicted that the American capture of British Canada would be "only a matter of marching." By the end of the war, Admiral Cockburn had destroyed and sacked the White House in retaliation for the American torching of what is now Toronto, and the Library of Congress had also gone up in flames. Jefferson offered to compensate this terrible loss by selling his personal collection in a letter to Maryland Congressman Samuel Harrison Smith. He requested $23,999 for this outstanding collection of 6,487 volumes. Some New England Federalists, including Massachusetts Congressman Cyrus King, scoffed at the deal, declaring: "It might be inferred, from the character of the man who collected it, and France, where the collection was made, that the library contained irreligious and immoral books, works of the French philosophers, who caused and influenced the volcano of the French Revolution." The law would put $23,999 in Jefferson's pocket for around 6,000 books, good, bad, and indifferent, old, new, and useless, in languages that many cannot read and should not."

If the bigoted and provincial King had studied Jefferson's classification and cataloguing system, he could have been even more enraged. He categorized literature according to the categories of "Memory," "Understanding," and "Imagination," taking his lead from Francis Bacon's 1605 essay The Advancement of Learning, and consistently placing the discussion of religion and ecclesiastical history at the bottom of the ladder of accomplishment. He'd done the same thing while advising his Virginia neighbor and in-law Robert Skipwith on the creation of a "gentleman's library," putting the Bible at the end of a long list of books labeled "Ancient History." In the end, Congress overruled Cyrus King and other protesters and paid the slightly lower sum of $23,950 for Jefferson's books. The collection and catalogue were the heart of the Library of Congress until a fire in 1851 destroyed two-thirds of it, satisfying many who had suspected it was the devil's work from the start. Today, the Library of Congress, with its centerpiece in the Jefferson Room, is one of the world's most magnificent public institutions.

Being assaulted for impiety was nothing new for Jefferson. His acquaintance with Thomas Paine, as well as his drafting of the Virginia Statute on Religious Freedom, had made the faithful aware of the possibilities of many forms of heresy. Even during election season, he did little to quell such sentiments. He wrote that it didn't matter whether a neighbor believed in no god or many gods, because such a personal belief "neither picks my pocket nor breaks my leg." The Christians found this laconic attitude repugnant, and their diatribes were met with coldness in return. During the 1800 election, Jefferson was attacked by Christian extremists and stated, "The returning good sense of our country threatens abortion to their hopes." They believe that any power given to me will be used in opposition to their plans. And they are correct; for I have sworn on God's altar perpetual war against any form of tyranny over man's thinking."

This pledge was made in a private letter to Dr. Benjamin Rush, one of Jefferson's most important and learned colleagues in the American Philosophical Society, so the mention of the "altar of God" cannot be attributed to any desire to avoid the politically lethal charge of atheism, as it has been with some of Jefferson's more public statements. Rush was both a rationalist and a materialist, but he was also a Deist. When Thomas Paine published The Age of Reason, he severed ties with him, whom he had persuaded to write Common Sense. Nonetheless, he was adamant about ridding Christianity of the superstitions and priestcraft that had engulfed it. He repeatedly asked Jefferson to clarify his own views on the subject. The president was tempted to blame it on other matters, but his mind was clearly on the subject, and he received additional impetus from the great Dr. Joseph Priestley, whose History of the Corruptions of Christianity, written before his exile from England, was one of Jefferson's favorite books. Following this, Priestley sent Jefferson his treatise Socrates and Jesus Compared, and the reading of this little piece in 1804 convinced Jefferson of a bigger scheme. He vowed to write about the life of Jesus, distinguishing fact from myth and allowing for legend's distortions and oral history's exaggerations, in order to arrive at anything resembling an ethical minimum. Indeed, Jefferson once stated that "there is not a young man now living in the United States who will not die a Unitarian," and while this may appear to be the most ridiculously wrong-headed prediction, there are many millions of educated Americans, Christian and Jewish, and of no particular denomination, who now hold views that are not dissimilar.

Jefferson admired Priestley so much that he thought it would be him who finished the mission of updating and reworking the Bible story. On his own account, he made a few stabs at the suggestion, pedantically titled "Syllabus of an estimate of the merit of the Doctrines of Jesus, compared with those of others." "Like Socrates and Epictetus, he wrote nothing himself"; "According to the ordinary fate of those who attempt to enlighten and reform mankind, he fell an early victim to the jealousy and combination of the altar and the throne"; "The doctrines which he really delivered were defective as a whole, and fragments only of what he did deliver have come to us mutilated, misstated, and often unintelligible." This was rather standard fare. And any greater projects were shelved after Priestley's death in 1805. Dr. Benjamin Rush, on the other hand, was to provide one final service. Disgusted by Jefferson and John Adams' protracted separation, he negotiated a reunion between the two men, who gradually resumed a communication that, as preserved, is one of the great epistolatory treasures of all time. The transaction began in 1812. By 1813, the year Rush died, Adams, who had learned of Jefferson's contact with Priestley, was writing to him, pleading with him to keep his commitment to write about religion.

The Philosophy of Jesus, published in 1805, was billed on the cover as "an abridgement of the New Testament for the use of the Indians, unembarrassed with matters of fact or faith beyond the level of their comprehensions." This certainly corresponded to Jefferson's belief that Indians should be protected from Christian missionaries, but some Unitarians speculate that it also provided him with a respectable cover story for his otherwise profane exercise of severing the holy book with a razor blade and discarding all superfluous, ridiculous, and devotional parts. (This is an activity I've long wished to perform in the instance of Dumas Malone's laboriously penned multivolume hagiography of Jefferson himself.)

The Life and Morals of Jesus of Nazareth, Extracted Textually from the Gospels, published as a parallel text in Greek, Latin, French, and English, is commonly referred to jokingly as "the Jefferson Bible." On the day of their inauguration, new members of the United States Senate were given a copy of the Constitution in 1904. The Unitarian Universalist Church places a high value on the book, and while it has not succeeded in capturing the majority of American males, as Jefferson expected, it did pioneer the practice of ordaining women many years ago. (With his general skepticism about women's suitability for serious office, Jefferson would probably not have approved of this step.)

As his days dwindled, Jefferson wrote to friends several times that he approached the end without hope or fear. This was tantamount to stating unequivocally that he was not a Christian. We must withhold judgment on whether he was an atheist, if only because of the prudence he was forced to use during his political career. However, as he wrote to his nephew Peter Carr in 1787, one should not "be frightened from this inquiry by any fear of its consequences." If it leads to the conclusion that there is no God, you will find incitements to virtue in the comfort and pleasure you experience in exercising it, as well as the affection of others that it will bring you."

In May 1824, an itinerant scholar and book salesman named Samuel Whitcomb paid a visit to Monticello and was greeted by Jefferson himself. Whitcomb was unable to persuade the eighty-one-year-old former president to buy a copy of Mitford's History of Greece, which Jefferson denounced as carrying insults against ancient Athenians. Whitcomb then turned to other topics and discovered that Jefferson said of "Negroes" that "he hopes well of their minds but has never seen evidence of genius among them," and of Indians that they "will all dwindle away and be lost in our race by amalgamation."

Jefferson took his final, pessimistic position on slavery at the same time he was finishing his task of radical biblical revisionism. In a letter to one of its authors, John Holmes, he said that the Missouri Compromise of 1820 had "awakened and filled me with terror like a fire bell in the night." It struck me as the death bell for the Union." The old warrior's knack for words had not faded. In the same letter, he said, "freeing slaves would not cost me a second thought if, in that way, a general emancipation and expatriation [emphasis original] could be effected; and, gradually, and with due sacrifices, I think it might be." But, as it is, we have the wolf by the ears and cannot safely hold him or let him go. On one scale, there is justice, and on the other, there is self-preservation." "I regret that I am now to die in the belief, that the useless sacrifice of themselves by the generation of 1776, to obtain self-government and happiness for their country, is to be thrown away by the unwise and unworthy passions of their sons, and that my only consolation is to live not to weep over it," he concluded. Jefferson's pain of self-pity, with its rare suggestion of senior tremulousness, also drove him to express himself in less beautiful ways, hardly indicating that "self-preservation" and "justice" were in equal proportion in his mind. In a letter to Adams, he screamed, "Are our slaves to be presented with freedom and a dagger?" Where would it all end if Congress could override the states on the issue of slavery, he asked Albert Gallatin? "All whites south of the Potomac and Ohio must evacuate their states; and the most fortunate are those who can do so first." A minor but telling incident shed light on his more general coarsening. Thaddeus Kosciusko, a Polish hero of the American Revolution who had been imprisoned under the Alien and Sedition Acts, had died in Switzerland in 1817.

He appointed Jefferson as his executor and bequeathed all of his money to a fund to purchase the freedom and education of young African slaves. The sage of Monticello politely declined to carry out his dying friend's dying wish. He devoted his efforts to the concept of "colonization," a euphemism for the exodus and resettlement of black Americans in Sierra Leone and Liberia.

Jefferson became increasingly despondent and choleric after joining what Virginian conservatives grandly dubbed a Republican rebirth and praising the work of dogmatic agricultural writers like his buddy John Taylor. After John Quincy Adams was elected over Andrew Jackson, he addressed a private letter to his old ally William Giles, who was now governor of Virginia, in which he rehashed all of his well-worn anti-Federalist cliches. "Having nothing in them of the principles of '76," he said, "they now look back to a single and splendid government of an aristocracy, founded on banking institutions and monied incorporations under the guise and cloak of their favored branches of manufactures, commerce, and navigation, riding and ruling over the plundered ploughman and beggared yeomanry." This was not the end of it. He said that the states should be on watch against the center, and that if the alternative is between "dissolution of our Union... or submission to a government without limitation of powers," the decision must be for secession. So it turned out that the big terrible (black) wolf had Jefferson by the ears. This letter to Giles was private, written in 1826 when Jefferson had just a few months to live, but Giles made it public after Jefferson's death, helping to form the moral basis for John Calhoun's "states' rights" doctrine.

In 1874, historian James Parton stated unequivocally, "If Jefferson was wrong, America is wrong." If America is correct, Jefferson was correct." This oft-quoted assertion fails as both an epigram and an aphorism. Leave aside whether a man or a nation may be "right." Allow for the folly of making a nation's or country's "rightness" dependant on an individual's rectitude. Forget that the "rights" declared by Americans are either inalienable or not, natural or not, and exist (or do not exist) independently of any man's choice or character. The truth is that America has both done grave wrongs and committed crimes while also upholding great values and beliefs. It is primarily an urban and capitalist society, but it is also notably rural or, as some prefer to call it, pastoral. It has both an imperial and an isolationist history. It has a secular constitution yet is extremely religious and pietistic. Jefferson is one of the few historical personalities whose absence cannot be imagined: his contribution to the expansion and defining of the United States is too significant, even at this distance, to be diminished by the passage of time. But all of the above tensions and contradictions, many of which he embodied and symbolized, would have existed even if he had never been born.

The word experiment, as used to describe the American Revolution in Jefferson's final public letter, has subsequently taken on a new and sinister connotation. Stalinist defenders liked to refer to their own system as "the great socialist experiment," and, like their ostensible Nazi adversaries, they did perform "experiments" on living human beings. (Not all Communists were as oblivious. When Ho Chi Minh issued Vietnam's declaration of independence in 1945, he followed the precedent of the Seneca Falls convention on women's rights and framed his preamble in Jefferson's own words.) The phrase "experiment," whether spoken or written by Jefferson, referred to the scientific curiosity of his American Philosophical Society colleagues: the humanistic genius of a Rittenhouse, Rush, Barton, or Priestley. The endeavor to be tried was self-government. The French Revolution annihilated itself during Jefferson's lifetime. More recent revolutions have annihilated themselves and others. If the American Revolution, with its secularism, separation of powers, Bill of Rights, and gradual enfranchisement of those excluded or worse at its founding, has frequently betrayed itself at home and abroad, it remains the only revolution with any power to inspire.

In the course of a long political career, Thomas Jefferson had amassed enough "multitudes," in Walt Whitman's word, to contradict himself with scope and compassion. He took positions on a wide range of issues, from government interference with the press to congressional control over spending, and from the retention of permanent armed forces to the continuation of overseas entanglements. In many of these occasions, his explanation for reversal or contradiction was the greater cause of the American

Republic's growth and power. It is not difficult to read the promptings of personal self-interest in a smaller number. In the end, his submission to a slave authority he despised was both self-serving and a threat to the republic's survival. This surrender by an Enlightenment man of truly revolutionary and democratic temperament is yet another reminder that history is a tragedy, not a morality play.

Printed in Great Britain
by Amazon

34248747R00050